D0148490

ELEKTRA

A PLAY BY EZRA POUND
AND RUDD FLEMING

ELEKTRA

· A PLAY BY ·
EZRA POUND AND RUDD FLEMING

EDITED AND ANNOTATED BY

Richard Reid

PRINCETON UNIVERSITY PRESS · PRINCETON, NEW JERSEY

PA
4414
.E5
P68
1989

Text of *Elektra* copyright © 1987, 1989
by the Trustees of the Ezra Pound Literary Property Trust and Rudd Fleming.
Introduction, Notes, and annotation copyright © 1989
by Princeton University Press.
Published by Princeton University Press, 41 William Street,
Princeton, New Jersey 08540.

All Rights Reserved.

Library of Congress Cataloging-in-Publication Data
Sophocles.
Elektra.
Translation of: Electra / Sophocles.
1. Electra (Greek mythology)—Drama. I. Pound,
Ezra, 1885–1972. II. Reid, Richard, 1953–
III. Title.
PA4414.E5P68 1989   882′.01   89-10247
ISBN 0-691-06778-3 (alk. paper)

This book has been composed in Linotron Zapf International

Clothbound editions of Princeton University Press books
are printed on acid-free paper, and binding materials are
chosen for strength and durability.
Printed in the United States of America by Princeton University Press,
Princeton, New Jersey.

FOR

RUDD AND POLLY FLEMING

BEAVER COLLEGE LIBRARY
GLENSIDE, PA. 19038

CONTENTS

INTRODUCTION

Deep into Pound's *Cantos*, in the section titled "Thrones," a reader stumbles across a very odd line. There, someone named "Yo-Yo," evidently the poet's fellow inmate at St. Elizabeths Hospital in Washington, D.C., utters this somewhat arresting question: "What part ob yu iz deh poEM??" Ostensibly, the poet is inviting us to consider the circumstances to which he has been reduced or, as he puts it, his present "vicinage" and his "peers." At the time of the line's composition, he remains under indictment for treason against the United States and hospitalized under court order. Perhaps, too, we are asked to consider, further, the impossibility that he could be given a fair trial when it has been determined already that he is fit for the company only of madmen. Yet I suspect there may be more involved in Pound's quotation, that poor Yo-Yo is not simply intended to be a foil against which the poet's preëminent sanity might shine. Nor is the line without its element of humor. Its tone of exaggerated mimicry is familiar to readers of Pound, as is its exuberant relish for the wriest of ironies. We may even hear that same Pound who was able to appreciate, in Book 5 of Homer's *Odyssey*, the comedy of Hermes' reply to Calypso when asked about the reason for his sudden descent from Olympos: "You, a goddess, ask *me*, a god." But the joke in Canto 104 might be rather: "you, a schizophrenic, or a manic-depressive, you, Yo-Yo, ask me, a poet?" That is to say, the poet quite distinctly reminds us of his immediate surroundings and of their legal repercussions. But he may be paying his interlocutor a backhanded compliment too, shrewdly acknowledging that the seemingly addlebrained query could well be worth our attending. For in lieu of the conventional biographical critic's tired inquiry, what part of the poem can be directly related to the author's private life, we are offered a refreshing alternative. Let us understand that the poetic work may be neither an adequate nor an uncomplicatedly reliable register of a life. And, what is more, let us acknowledge that in his verses the poet may turn upon the man, may be in fact at odds, very violently, with himself.

I have belabored this initial point because a poetry such as Pound's understandably invites biographical speculations. How else are we to come to terms with the myriad recorded bits of conversation and other personal reminiscences that consort on his pages with quoted fragments from, and allusions to, a virtual entirety of our written past? We cannot easily take it as mere coincidence, for example, that the *Cantos* begin with a truncated rendering of *Odyssey* 11, a visitation to the dead, and with a very specific reference to the poet's Latin source, a Renaissance translation he once retrieved along a Parisian quay. The founding myth and the myth of the found artifact are intimately meshed. And they both concern the mysteries of the translator's heroic and eternally baffled undertaking. In its triple-layered structure, Pound engaging Divus engaging Homer, Canto 1 stunningly refigures the heartbreaking gesture of Odysseus' own thrice-missed embrace in Hades, an image of the inevitable futility in the effort to recover a beloved shade out of death's muted kingdom. The image is a tragic one, and in Pound's hands it becomes an image of translation itself. Canto 1 marks for Pound yet another, if more ambitious, *persona*, one more mask. A mask of course disguises. It manifests, yes, but conceals just the same. In the act of translation we discover the poet speaking with a necessarily "forked tongue," as it were, in a voice one's own and not one's own. It is no wonder, then, that we accept the Italian pun, *traduttore/traditore*, translator/traitor, as a very matter-of-fact expression of the translator's art. And it is translation, above all, that preoccupies Pound's poetic career from beginning to end.

We shall want, therefore, to tread warily in turning to Pound's translations from Greek tragedy, in particular to this "new" version of Sophocles' *Elektra*. For it too is integral to the poet's life and to the life of his long poem. That Pound's *Elektra* is hardly new, in fact, goes without saying, nor should it have come to us as any real surprise, despite the fact that it remained out of cir-

culation for nearly forty years, till it was invigoratingly per-
formed in the autumn of 1987 by Carey Perloff's Classic Stage
Company in New York. We know that Pound's affinities for the
myth of the House of Atreus date at least to a series of articles he
wrote for *The Egoist* in 1918 and 1919, on translations of Homer
and Aeschylus. It was during this postwar period that he con-
ceived, too, the project of translating the *Agamemnon* and tried
initially to enlist T. S. Eliot for the "job." The story of that aborted
effort gets somewhat lost in the margins of the Pound–Eliot let-
ters that deal with *The Waste Land*. But Pound mentioned it
again in 1938, in *Guide to Kulchur*: "I asked Eliot to have a shot
at the *Agamemnon*. He didn't. Or rather he sat on it for eight
months or some longer period. I then took over." ("I would have
sent Aeschule before," Eliot had written in 1922, *annus mirabi-
lis*, "but have been in bed with flu.") In any event, the few sur-
viving pages of Pound's version amount to a condensed, lugu-
briously ironic, heavy-handed indictment of imperial Christendom
and of war:

> Parson: Let us give thanks unto Jupiter
> King of gods, for the beautiful evening, and for
> our victory over the Trojans,
> let us express our gratitude   , that Paris has
> been punished for his sins   , and his immoralities,
>
> and for killing Achilles.

So much for the hundred and forty lines of the second stasimon.
The poet himself finally admitted that "the translation is unread-
able." And perhaps we may hear an even more powerfully condensed rendering in the postwar outrage of *Mauberley*: "came
home, home to a lie/ home to many deceits/ home to old lies and
new infamy." Eliot, too, was eventually to compose his own *Agamemnon* of sorts, *Murder in the Cathedral*.

It was Eliot himself who first gave us our clue that Pound's
interest in Greek tragedy had extended beyond Aeschylus alone.
In the introduction to his edition of Pound's *Literary Essays*
(1954), Eliot parenthetically remarked the fact that the poet-
critic "ignores consideration of dramatic verse." "Quite rightly,"

Eliot added—almost admonishingly? one wonders—quite rightly, because Pound would not write about a form of verse "which he would not care to practice."* It is in fact true that Pound himself repeatedly expressed his lack of interest in drama and, with the exception of his collaboration with Yeats on Fenollosa's *noh* materials and his constant praise of Cocteau's plays, he seemed always to speak of the theater as if it were an affair of footlights, tenors, and rouge. Yet an editor's footnote to Pound's discussion of Athens' "great dramatists" in "How to Read" ("The 'great dramatists' decline from Homer . . . Even Æschylus is rhetorical") gave a hint of what Eliot knew was to come: "E. P.'s later and unpublished notes, revise all this in so far as they demand much greater recognition of Sophokles." Naturally, with the nearly simultaneous publication of Pound's *Women of Trachis* in the *Hudson Review* and the subsequent performance of the play over the BBC in the spring of 1954, Eliot's note appeared to have been accounted for.

But five years earlier Pound had written an *Elektra*, too. Having met a young visitor to St. Elizabeths, a professor at the University of Maryland named Rudd Fleming, whose unpublished novel based on the legend of Agamemnon recommended him as a prospective co-worker, Pound was encouraged in his renewed preoccupation with things Greek, with tragic drama in particular, and now with the plays of Sophocles. If we rely on a brief contemporaneous memorandum Pound wrote in February or March of 1949, titled "Hellenists," we see that his hopes were ultimately for nothing less than a total Greek "revival": a complete set of translations in cheap, bilingual editions. These were to be translations that could be "*sung*." They would recognize, formally, that in the metrical syncopation to be learned from Greek choral lyrics resided the very "life of verse" and recognize, thematically, that in the Greek drama itself appeared the "rise of [a] sense of civic responsibility." To be realized anew, Pound felt, was that virtue he had earlier claimed for Cocteau's *Antigone*: a

* We have been recently reminded that, in 1916, the poet at least had tried to make himself into a playwright. See Donald Gallup's edition of Pound's *Plays Modelled on the Noh* (Toledo: The Friends of the University of Toledo Libraries, 1987).

contemporary language charged with the "*whole political wisdom*" of our own time. So, taking responsibility upon himself, he would point the way for yet another generation of translators from the Greek. But—his translation would appear under Rudd Fleming's name. Mr. Fleming has explained that because of the precarious legal situation, Pound did not wish it to appear that he was "sane" enough to translate Greek. And of course an *Elektra* by Pound would provide the Feds with their *Q.E.D.* The anecdote is a telling one.

The choice, too, of Sophocles' *Elektra* instead of, say, the *Libation Bearers* of Aeschylus is equally revealing. That is, in yet another postwar period, why should Pound not pursue his earlier interest in the *Oresteia* and just reëmphasize the destructiveness and futility of a seemingly endless series of bloody recriminations? For such would have been consistent with his proclaimed view of both the first and second World Wars, that indeed the history of our century continued what is a single perennial war interrupted by the mere "parenthesis of peace," as he put it. Perhaps so, but to follow upon the *Agamemnon* with a *Libation Bearers* would be to imply the third play of the Aeschylean trilogy, the *Eumenides*, and the recuperative energies that compelled its strange vision into the historical present of fifth-century, democratic Athens. As Bernard Knox has suggested in *The Heroic Temper*, Sophocles' eschewal of the trilogy in favor of a single play might be interpreted as one way of ruling out the future. And to a poet for whom the future is very much in doubt, and a trial by jury obviated, Sophocles could well prove the safer bet. Yet, one may be also reminded of what Nabokov once remarked in an essay called "The Tragedy of Tragedy": "The effect of a play cannot be final when it ends with murder." For Pound, in 1949, the future was very decidedly unresolved, but equally so was the immediate past. There remained a good deal of unfinished business: the *Cantos*, for instance, in their apparent demise after the poetry composed at Pisa. What was to become of the poem, the life's work, the fate of which had grown so intimately annexed to that of Mussolini's now-fallen Rome?

The *Cantos* themselves testify to the abiding importance of Sophocles' *Elektra* for Pound. At least four references to the play, all of them transcribed in Greek, riddle the pages of the section published in 1955 under the title *Rock Drill*. Near the close of Canto 85 we read: "Jury trial was in Athens./ Tyrants resisted/ οὐ ταῦτα . . . κακοῖσι δειλίαν." And again in the next canto: "All, that has been, is as it should have been, / but what will they trust in/ now?/ . . . / 'Alla non della', in the Verona statement/οὐ ταῦτα . . . κακοῖσι." Included in this latter passage is a Chinese ideogram that reminds us of "fidelity to the given word," of "man standing by his word." It suggests as well the degree to which Pound's reading of the *Elektra* and, even more obviously, the *Trachiniae* was influenced by his own Confucianism. We have, then, some Chinese, some Italian, some Greek, and Pound as ever translating into and out of his native English tongue, in search of the proper word to stand by. The repeated Greek phrase derives from Sophocles' play, from the initial confrontation between Elektra and her sister Chrysothemis. The latter has just agreed that Elektra is essentially right in her unmitigated wrath, but has proposed a "pragmatic" approach toward coping with the sisters' troubles: bow down to the powers that be in order to maintain one's freedom—or at least one's life. (This is not wholly inconsistent with the hoped-for efficacy of an insanity plea.) Elektra retorts, in Pound's translation: "Need we add cowardice to all the rest of this filth?" A very similar translation ("this filth" changed to "these ills") appears in a footnote toward the end of Pound's *Women of Trachis*, in which the translator claims that Elektra's words are the "key phrase" of the play. And in that same footnote we discover the original Italian that Pound translates in Canto 86, "All, that has been, is as it should have been" (or variously, in Canto 87, "What has been, should have"). These words, given without any ascription either in Italian or in English, derive from a memoir attributed to Mussolini, from the period following his downfall in July of 1943. Unsurprisingly, the three Italian words allude to a statement by Mussolini as well, made at Verona after the establishment of the new Salò Republic. There his insistence was that housing was a matter concerning not just the right *of* property but also the right *to* property, a nicety in distinction that Pound had already appreciated in the "Pisan Cantos."

The next reference to the *Elektra* occurs in Canto 89, two words only, "κατὰ σφαγάς," given in relation to another Italian,

Giuseppe Mazzini, and to his primer of ethics "On the Duties of Man." But these words have no real cogency without the context of Pound's translation—or, in this instance, his mistranslation. For Pound has construed Sophocles' Greek to mean that Agamemnon had slain the stag of Artemis in violation of established "hunting rites." Agamemnon was thus placed (as similarly Mazzini would be confounded by the political history of his day) in a tragic dilemma, compelled to sacrifice Iphigeneia "against his own nature," according to Pound. Finally, in Canto 90, Elektra herself makes an appearance, her name recorded just as we find it in Sophocles: "and the dark shade of courage/ Ἠλέκτρα/ bowed still with the wrongs of Aegisthus." "Aegisthus," Pound writes, not "Klytemnestra." But even more intriguingly, more significantly, Elektra is *still* bowed, as if the murders of Aegisthus and Klytemnestra had accomplished nothing after all. In the *Cantos* she is just among a whole host of shades out of "Erebus," that vicinage of Canto 1, among the ascending remnants only of a "dream" that has not been abandoned by the poet.*

Now, what emerges from the sundry fragments in the *Cantos* is a Poundian ideogram of sorts, a constellation of the poet's deepest convictions and worries. On the one hand, we seem to have a stubborn dedication to maintaining the courage of one's convictions, to standing by one's "word." On the other, there rings a finally tragic affirmation of utter failure in the face of an inexorable history. And between these two extremities there is juggled the troubling question of "rights"—legal and economic rights—but also the profounder question: where lies justice itself amid all the conflicting claims to rightness? Finally, all these issues are communicated through a series of translations, or quotations, that are repeated—but never precisely in the same terms. And we are left to consider the possibility that the "mot juste" may remain forever elusive and that, certainly, the very definition of "justice" must hang in the balance yet.

So much as this, in any case, seems near to the heart of Sopho-

* I strongly suspect that Pound's own Italian Canto 73, written in Italy's most anxious days during World War II, further disposed him to the story of Elektra. For in that poem a young Italian girl, aided by her brother, takes revenge against rapacious Canadian troops who have invaded her "fatherland" and leads them all through a live mine field to their doom. She is herself destroyed.

cles' tragedy and may well suggest its deep allure for Pound. This
is not to deny, of course, the immediate attraction for the poet to
the figure of Elektra herself. The most tender moments in
Pound's translation are consigned to the lamenting voice of Elektra. In the central choral dialogue between her and the Women
of Mycenae, the lyrical tone evokes the quietude of hurt and nos-
talgia reminiscent of *Cathay* (Elektra, much like the translator,
is an "Exile" in her own homeland). The rhetoric of repetition
anticipates the unembarrassed modulations of internal rhyme
and end rhyme that inform the *Confucian Odes*. And, here, it
reenacts the precedent of the Greek itself (*istôr, hyperistôr,/ pan-
surtôi pammênoi*), a language of empirical exacerbations, a
schooling of hard knocks by which one is educated into a knowl-
edge of pain:

> Known, dont I know, over known,
> day after day, moon over moon,
> overfull, pain over pain
> horrors of hate abate not
> ever.

Similarly, Elektra's response to the supposed ashes of her brother
Orestes, in Pound's version "Elektra's Keening," becomes a re-
lentless succession of "Sapphics" stripped to their final half-lines:
"sorrow upon me . . . fruitless my caring." Pound's stage directions for choral songs in the play insist upon a constant counter-
point between English and the original Greek. And the work as a
whole aims at a like tension of tonalities. If at moments the
translation seems to presume upon the provinces of Samuel Beck-
ett ("nothing to be DONE AMEXANON about it . . . . . But I
must go on./ DEAD, he is dead, I must go on"), the tone of
Poundian high invective also registers itself, and often, in the dia-
logues of the play, as when Elektra reports the kind of verbal
abuse she has received from her mother Klytemnestra:

> You the only only slut ever lost a father,
> nobody else has any troubles,
> go rot and keep on yowling in hell.

Despite such felicities (and I think we should understand an

Elektra pitched, as she is here, so violently against herself as well
as against Klytemnestra), the translation nonetheless suffers
from many of the same willful eccentricities discovered in
Pound's *Women of Trachis*. Like that play, the *Elektra* amounts
to a bizarre amalgam of discourses: transliterated Greek, jazzy
slang, archaic English lyricism, Scots and Cockney and apparently Black American dialects, stage directions that allude to a
noh-like rarification of sensibility and then to a "wild Sioux injun
war dance with tommy hawks." Such a poetry, in essence, marks
the grotesque realization of what Pound termed "logopoeia,"
that "most tricky and undependable mode": "The dance of the
intellect among words." As Pound describes "logopoeia," it is the
"risk of using the word in some special relation to 'usage', that
is, to the kind of context in which the reader expects, or is accus-
tomed, to find it." The concept might be understood in part by
our notion of irony or wit, a volatile mode of writing, and one
that is likely at any moment to get out of hand and direct itself,
mercilessly, against the user. Because this kind of poetry, in its
jarring play of allusion, of contextuality and intertextuality,
seems to be without any sustained center of consciousness, we
would be wrong, I think, to attempt locating that center in the
character of Elektra alone. To view the *Elektra* in such a way
could be as reductive as seeing simply in the *Women of Trachis*
Pound's identification with a hero who cheats on his wife. How
then would we reconcile the macho poet with one who now sees
himself in the rags of a wretched girl? Perhaps some remarks
made on Pound's *Trachiniae* by the late Richmond Lattimore,
though not intended to be particularly generous criticism, may
be of some help here. Pound's Deianeira, Lattimore wrote, speaks
as a "brassy, cocksure guttersnipe." In fact, he added, "all the
other characters speak the same way." Nonetheless, something
along these lines might be instructively said of the *Elektra*, too.
Through the exacerbations of Pound's language we may recognize not just a Sophoclean play about a house divided, but also
one about language at war with itself, one in which all the antagonists seem implicated in its tragedy. And the translator assumes all roles with an equal vehemence.

All of Pound's characters, for instance, share with the poet a preoccupation with a "job" to be done, a "good job" or a "big job"—this seemingly beyond even the emphasis Sophocles gives to the word *ergon* at the outset of the drama. Nearly all of them speak on some occasion in very Poundian intonations of being "on the right track" or "on the wrong track." The Paidagogus, Pound's "Tutor," could be the "do as I say" professor of the "Ezuversity" instructing his charges, "be clear in your own mind what you're up to," or pointing out Mycenae, "center of the gold trade." The Tutor even salutes Klytemnestra with the words "Gruss Gott," an echo from a passage in the "Pisan Cantos" concerning the time when the poet himself was a messenger bearing ill tidings to his daughter in the north of Italy. Even Klytemnestra and the Chorus, too, seem to share a Poundian knowingness about the facts of conspiratorial intrigue: utterance time and again attains the cryptic force of a *trobar clus*. Or contrarily, Chrysothemis screams out in a gnomic, Poundian upper-case: "EVEN JUSTICE CAN BE A PEST."

The instances abound. The voice of the poet rings throughout the many various voices of the play, and perhaps in none more so than Orestes'. It is he who imagines his return from exile as the return of the "old rule of abundance." It is he who has interpreted his charge from Apollo's oracle in this way: "Dont start a war/ take a chance, do it yourself:/ Kinky course, clean in the kill." This "kinky course" refers to the deceit, thievish trickery and secrecy (*dolos, kleptein, kryptein* are Sophocles' words), to the specious story or *logos* he will have recourse to in order to effect the play's translation, as Pound might have it, of "ideas into action." He will pretend to be dead. Where is the pain in that, he wonders, what *lupê*? "I dont mind being dead that way," Pound translates, "if I can live on into honour." But we may be, just here, at the very crux of the play for the poet, the poet who found it imperative to translate Sophocles' tragedy while pretending to be, if not dead, insane, assuming like Orestes an incognito. There is something gravely disturbing in both Sophocles' and Pound's acknowledgment that the *logos* can be so readily divorced from the realm of veracity. In the cinerary urn that serves as a token to confirm the story of Orestes' "death," we find the alarming image itself of the tension between truth and falsehood in the poets' inventions and representations. And this image should enforce our sense of the operative deception at the core of translating from ancient Greek: the living play dead, so that the dead may be quickened. This sacrificial rite is not an altogether happy mystery. It appears, certainly, to be intimately at one with the essence of tragedy. In Orestes' climactic words to Aegisthus, "Haven't you ever learned/ that the DEAD dont DIE," we just may hear Pound's heartfelt assertion of the translator's credo, but also a ghastly exhortation and encouragement to carry through upon an enterprise of brutal ruthlessness.

The full frustration of a burdensome ambivalence seems expressed in some of Orestes' very last words to Aegisthus, when he imputes a universal significance to this specific act of vengeance: "It's a pity you cant all of you die like this," Pound translates, in a line that uncannily recalls his own early judgments upon the antagonists of the first World War. By the close of the second war, however, the seductive simplicity of that reasoning had become for Pound, too, tragically untenable.

I have to think, then, that the translation of the *Elektra* marks the poet's first, tentative reëxamination of his own and of the *Cantos'* role in history. In making explicit a tragic dimension first felt in the "Pisan Cantos," it acknowledges at the same time, very reluctantly, an impasse in the long poem, a fatal disjunction: the poem's alienation from a history of which it had presumed to make a privileged record. The time that its music measured had, within the time that history keeps, for all practical purposes stopped. How then was the poetic *ethos* to survive the calamitous *mythos* of history, and how was the poet's word, his *logos*, to be translated into the time of its contradiction? Perhaps only through a cautious, retrospective reading of Canto 1 can we realize that such a contradiction lay inherent in the poem from its very start. Still, I would suggest that Pound gives us a further clue in the *Elektra*, this drama of revenge set in motion by embittered love, misunderstanding, deception, and compromised heroism, a clue toward appreciating the course by which the *Cantos* were to be resumed in "Rock Drill" and "Thrones." In place of a poetry with an overarching will to "include" history, we can discover one that is increasingly conspiratorial, secretive, and ever more cryptically composed in the margins of history, a poetry that courts in fact the further reaches of silence.

In my passing references to the various characters of *Elektra*, I have omitted perhaps a very singular case, one whom Pound's Tutor refers to early on as "Mr. Pilades, stranger in these parts." And among the parts in this or any other play, that of Pylades is exceedingly strange indeed. Toward the end of his *Elektra*, one of Pound's stage directions remarks that Pylades "hasn't said a damn word." Orestes immediately, then, urges his comrade on to their bloody task: "Come on, Pylades, cut the cackle." Although this spectral, unnerving figure seems to be dismissed here with a joke, I think it fair to say that the significance of Pylades, as a presence transcending or just denied the vexed condition of human speech, was not entirely lost on Pound. For he was to appropriate, belatedly, that last persona, the dumb eloquence of Pylades, witness and abettor of horrors, of a tragedy too unspeakable for words. Maybe silence is, after all, that which gets lost in translation. And we have only Pound's late, implacable silence as a final gesture toward some recompense for the blasted efforts of a lifetime.

I shall only revert in concluding to that memorable phrase by which Pound qualified his heroine Elektra, "the dark shade of courage." I would hope, above all, that it might serve to remind us that the word "courage" has at its root what we call "heart," that quality Robert Lowell claimed Pound possessed to such a surpassing degree. And I would like to think that what Pound finally meant by the word was that courage which permitted him to carry on his *Cantos*, beyond the desire for revenge, into their last "Drafts & Fragments." The puzzled hauntings of Sophocles' tragedy discover perhaps their best translations there: "That love can be the cause of hate,/ something is twisted." "And as to why they go wrong,/ thinking of rightness." "Nor begins nor ends anything." Implied too in those fragments, after some fifty years, as if a finally recognized omen, are the lines so presciently translated into the early "Exile's Letter":

> What is the use of talking, and there is no end of
> talking.
> There is no end of things in the heart.

A NOTE ON THE TEXT

I have taken it as my principal editorial task to retain as much as possible what Pound continually referred to as the "provisional" nature of his translation. Quite obviously, the poet and his collaborator intended to make major revisions, especially of the choral lyrics. But these were not to be. At the expense of those intentions, then, I have refrained from making many of those ameliorations that would seem incumbent upon an editor of good will. My faithfulness to the historical documents includes the transmission of simple misspellings ("Pelop's" or "wreathes," for instance) and of inconsistencies in punctuation. Realizing, however, that a slavish fidelity to Pound's typographical anarchy might be in itself an inconsistency, I have taken some liberties in imposing order upon the manuscripts.

Chief among these is a systematization of the names of characters in the play. Klytemnestra, to take one example, assumes in Pound's hands such various guises as "KLUTAIMNESTRA," "Klut," "Klyt," "KL/," "Cl," "Clyt," "Clty," and so on. And it is the same with all the others, the "XO," "KHO," "Xopos," "Chorus" included. Because these numerous aliases seem to me functions not of an ideology but of a hurried shorthand, I have decided to dispense with them. Second, I have in extended passages regularized the transliterations of Greek indicated by Pound (retaining only his preference for representing *omega* by "OO"). Pound himself may have wished to print the actual Greek, but because he himself transliterated, with a surprising inventiveness, and because he seemed primarily concerned that actors be given the "sound" or the "music," I have kept to the Roman alphabet. Pound, unquestionably, would have included far more Greek, but this text complies only with his very specific instructions. Finally, I have enumerated the lines of the text throughout, giving equal value to the poet's often engaging stage directions, and I have generally presented them flushed to the left-hand margin. In the cause of fidelity, my alternative would have been to print them vertically, diagonally, and sometimes upside down. The running-head numbers correspond to lines of Greek in the Loeb edition.

The apparatus at the page bottoms provides preliminary and rejected versions of the translation at particular lines. The abbreviation **TMS** represents Pound's typed manuscript, and **FC**, the fair copy typed by Rudd Fleming. Pound made handwritten revisions and comments on both manuscripts, and these I have given in brackets. To the degree to which I could determine, all these "variants" appear in the order of their original composition, earliest to last. Because I can fully appreciate, and sympathize with, the difficulties Professor Fleming must have faced in making his own transcription, I have sometimes found it necessary to second-guess his choices in determining my "final" selections for the text proper. It seems evident to me that Pound often forgot or ignored his later reworkings in **TMS** when he read over first, tentative efforts transcribed into **FC**. Of course, where Pound's markings in the latter indicate that his attention has been newly and fully given to a line, I have accepted it as definitive.

The Notes that follow the text, it is hoped, will supplement and enrich the apparatus by reconstructing the ongoing "dialogue" conducted by Pound and Fleming in the margins of their typescripts. Although less than exhaustive, they indicate many of the difficulties, motives, and intertextual considerations at play in Pound's attempt to render Sophocles' often intractable Greek. It is certain, judging only from the books retained in Pound's library at Brunnenburg, that he had access to the following texts for assistance in his task: a 1939 edition of the Loeb *Sophocles*, vol. 2; an English translation of Ellendt's *A Lexicon to Sophocles*, abridged (Oxford: D. A. Talboys, 1841); and a copy of Jebb's *The Tragedies of Sophocles: Translated into English Prose* (Cambridge: Cambridge University Press, 1905). These, however, may not have been all. Although the passing of so many years has inevitably clouded the question, Professor Fleming is nonetheless certain that he at least worked from a copy of Jebb's bilingual edition with commentary, *Sophocles: The Plays and Fragments*,

Part 6 (Cambridge: 1894). But Pound's frequent queries as to Jebb's commentary suggest that he himself did not possess it in the early months of 1949 while at work on the *Elektra*. His only explicit reference to any other text at hand is to Goodwin's *A Greek Grammar*. In addition to documenting such matters as these, the Notes finally attempt to suggest instances where certain preoccupations of Pound's work on Sophocles may have been carried over from, or into, other of his writings. Clearly, they do not presume to be comprehensive.

There remains only for me to express my sincere gratitude to those who have helped me in preparing this edition. I wish above all to thank Rudd and Polly Fleming for their gracious, repeated hospitality and for so generously sharing their recollections of their friendship with Pound. I am deeply grateful as well to A. Walton Litz for his gesture of confidence in first recommending this project to me. And there are the others whose support has been appreciated no less: John Logan of the Firestone Library at Princeton; Robert Brown and Cathie Brettschneider of Princeton Univesity Press, who have so ably and expeditiously seen this through to print; Carey Perloff, who enlightened me not only with her production of the play but by providing me, too, a copy of her acting text; Froma Zeitlin, Yopie Prins, and Wendy Stallard Flory, all of whom responded instructively and kindly to an earlier version of the Introduction; William Mullen, Robert Kelly, and Noel Stock, who helped me to cut through some considerable *cruces*; my colleagues and the administration at Bard College, who supplied me with a research grant; and, by no means least, Juliana Mary Spahr, who worked with me and eased the strains of what looked at moments to be an editor's nightmare dreamed by Nabokov.

ELEKTRA

**A PLAY BY EZRA POUND
AND RUDD FLEMING**

DRAMATIS PERSONAE

TUTOR   *to Orestes*

ORESTES   *son of Agamemnon and Klytemnestra*

ELEKTRA   *daughter of Agamemnon and Klytemnestra*

CHORUS   *of Mycenean women*

CHRYSOTHEMIS   *sister of Elektra and Orestes*

KLYTEMNESTRA   *Queen of Argos and widow of Agamemnon*

AEGISTHUS   *Klytemnestra's lover and accomplice*

PYLADES   *silent friend to Orestes*

Scene: *at Mycenae, in front of Agamnenon's palace*

TUTOR

Well, here's where your father landed when he
got back from the Trojan war, this is where you
wanted to come to;
Old Argos over there
5   where the gad-fly chased Miss Inachus,
and that's the Lukeum, named after the wolf-god,
the wolf-killer, market place now;
and Hera's church on the left
everybody's heard about that.
10   Down below there: Mycene,
centre of the gold trade,
and Pelop's palace, the throne room
where the dirty murder was done.
That's where I picked you off your dad's
15   bloody body,
that is to say your kind sister
did, and give you to me to take off and raise
like a proper avenger.

And now, Orestes, it's up to you
20   and your dear friend Mr Pilades, stranger in these parts.
Get goin' quickly.
Sun's risin', birds are a singin',
stars going down, darkness broken,
Get going before people start moving about
25   and be clear in your own minds what you're up to.

ORESTES

All right, old Handy,
you sure have stuck with us
like a good ole horse rarin' for battle,
urgin' on and keepin' right forward
30   up in front every time.

This is what we're agoin' to do,
listen sharp and check up if
I miss any bullseyes.

When I went off to the Pythoness
35   to ask about doin' right by my father
Phoebus answered:

Dont start a war,
take a chance, do it yourself:
Kinky course, clean in the kill.

40   Now as that's the oracle that we heard
the first chance you get
you nip into this building, find out everything that's
going on there, and keep us wise to the lot of it. Snap.
Nobody'll recognize your old block
45   after all these years, under all this herbage
Make yr cock-crow
You've come here from their best pal Phanoteus
first time you've ever been out of Phocia.
Swear that Orestes was killed in a chariot race
50   at the Pythians. Put in the details.

We'll go to dad's tomb, as ordered
with libations an' all my pretty curls
we'll bring back that nice brass urn
we hid in the underbrush
55   to back up the yarn that I'm dead
and buried
and this dust all that is left of me.
They'll like that.

32 TMS check me, correct me/ **33 TMS** anywhere off centre/ **34 TMS** pythian medium/ **35 TMS** for settling up father's murder; right way/licit on killers; what was permissable to do to the killers, cd/ do; to learn/ **39 TMS** twisty, stealthy [sneaky], but a just [due] kill; [Twisty but the kill's to be made (killing is to be)]; [Sneaky, but the kill(ing) is due]; [a sneak's trick, but the kill is due]/ **41 FC** *omits this line*/ **44 TMS** your white top/ **45 TMS** in that costume; or suspect that get-up; (? takes hold of T's long hair??); **FC** (takes hold of TUTOR's long hair)/ **46 TMS** use word; Pitch a tale under rights of hospitium/ **47 TMS** ex-enemy & best/ **50 TMS** build up the details/ **51 TMS** (permitted, proper??)/ **65f FC** *omits these lines*/ **67ff.**

60   I dont mind being dead that way
     if I can live on into honour.
     I dont suppose the lie will ruin our luck
     not the first time a wise guy
     has said he was dead
     in order to get a warm welcome;
65   and if it lets me bust out afterward
     and explode 'em.

     Earth of the fatherland
     bless the roads we have come by
     for the old home and this clean up,
70   the gods are in me to do this,
     clean the old home
     that I be not sent back into exile dishonoured
     give back the heritage
     that I bring back the old rule of abundance
75   and make it solid.

     Nuff talk. Get in there, old buck, and
     keep steady
     We'll be out here and watch for the moment,
     the time.
80   Best leader men have.

ELEKTRA

Oh, oh, I'm so unhappy.

TUTOR

Some slavey howling, inside there

TMS Gods help us, let the local gods help us/ and put thru this job/ let the old home be clean again,/ for the gods are in me to do this,/ **77 TMS** keep watch when you're in there; watch yr/ step when you've got there; the necessary; get in there and watch and do whatever's got to be done./ **78 TMS** and we'll watch the chance outside; **FC** and we'll (go now)/ **79f TMS, FC** time, time the best leader/ **81 TMS** miserable *deleted*/ **82 TMS** (sobbing) crying suppressed voice,; **FC** (sobbing, crying, suppressed

ORESTES

Poor Elektra, might be,
wanna stay and listen?

TUTOR

85   Certainly not. Get our bearings first
as Loxias ordered. Holy water to wash up
the tomb-stone.
That's the way to win out.

ELEKTRA

OO PHAOS HAGNON
90   Holy light
Earth, air about us,
                         THRENOON OODAS
                         POLLAS D'ANTEREIS AESTHOU
tearing my heart out
95   when black night is over
all night already horrible
been with me
my father weeping
there in that wretched house
100   weeping his doom
Not killed abroad in the war
but by mother and her bed-boy Aegisthus.
Split his head with an axe as
a woodcutter splits a billet of oak,
105   and that killed him
and nobody else in this house seems to mind.
Well I'm not going to forget it
and the stars can shine on it, all of them
tears of hate
110   all flaming rips of the stars
tide

voice)/ **83 TMS** Porr Electra/ **88 FC** (Some movement of Orestes is probably
stopped by the Tutor)/ **89 TMS** PAHOS AGNON/ **94 TMS** beating/ **107 FC** (anti-

destiny
and the day can look on it
I wont stand it and just keep quiet

115   ALL' OU MEN DE
                       LAEXOO THRENOON
You cant stop a nightingale crying, for her young, or me
on this house porch
let everyone hear it

120   Hell and Persephone
                    OO DOOM' AIDOU
OO CHTHONI' Hermes, Oh Queen of Avenging
                    ARA, O Vengeance
Hear me

125   ye that watch over shed blood,
over murder, over the usurping of beds
CURSE, and hear me
god seed, ye Erinnys, of doom
aid and defend us, avenging our father's death

130   HAI TOUS ADIKOOS THNEISKONTAS HORATH'
HAI TOUS EUNAS HUPOKLEPTOMENOUS
ELTHET' AREXATE TISASTHE PATROS
PHONON HEMETEROU
KAI MOI TON EMON PEMPSAT' ADELPHON

135   MOUNE GAR AGEIN OUKETI SOOKOO
LUPES ANTIRROPON ACHTHOS

(sinks onto step)

and
send me my brother
I can do no more on my own

140   this grief is too heavy

---

systema)/ **117 TMS** cant stop nightengale [*sic*]; **FC** you cant stop nightingale
[crying]/ **118 TMS** on the porch; this house porch; **FC** on the porch/ **119 TMS**
PASI/ **122 TMS** O XTHonoan Hermes; **FC** OO XTHONOIAN HERMES/ **130ff**
TMS AI TOUS ADIKOOS THNESKONTAS HORATH/ AI TOUS EUNAS HUPO-
KLEPTOMENOUS/ Elt/ PH/ to end/ of gk/ **137 FC** [&° in exhausted voice/ change of

CHORUS

OO PAI PAI DUSTANOTATAS
ELEKTRA MATROS TIN' AEI
TAKEIS OOD' AKORESTON OIMOOGAN
TON PALAI EK DOLERAS ATHEOOTATA

145   MATROS HALONT' APATAIS AGAMEMNONA
KAKAI TE CHEIRI PRODOTON HOOS HO TADE
    POROON
OLOIT' EI MOI THEMIS TAD' AUDAN

Poor Elektra
you had a curse for a mother
150   and are withered with weeping,
Agamemnon was tricked and murdered.
That was a long time ago,
but a dirty hand did it, maternal,
and to breed their destruction
155   if my deem is heard in dooming.
               EI MOI THEMIS TAD' AUDAN

ELEKTRA (quasi sotto voce)

Yes, you are come nobly to help me,
I can feel that,
But I must go on.
160   DEAD, he is dead, I must go on
OO GENETHLA GENNAIOON
HEKET' EMOON KAMATOON PARAMUTHION
OIDA TE KAI XUNIEMI TAD' OU TI ME
PHUNGANEI OUD' ETHELOO PROLIPEIN TODE
165   ME OU TON EMON STENACHEIN PATER' ATHLION
ALL' OO PANTOIAS PHILOTETOS AMEIBOMENAI
    CHARIN
EATE M' OOD' ALUEIN
AIAI HIKNOUMAI

---

tone]/ **141ff TMS** XO/ 7 lines gk/ **160f TMS** I appreciate your kind feelings and reciprocate; and . . . . . reciprocate/ **161ff TMS** 8 lines Gk (to Xo)/ **169 FC** [It's my

> *(to Chorus)* It's my job,

170　I have never asked to neglect it
　　let me go on alone

CHORUS

　　But you wont get him back out of black hell
　　by praying and groaning,
　　you wear yourself out with too much of it,
175　no harm to let up for a little

　　(emphatic and explicit with meaning to ram it in)

　　ALL' OU TOI G' EX AÏDA
　　PANKOINOU LIMNAS PATER' AN-
　　STASEIS OUTE GOOISIN OUT' EUCHAIS
180　ALL' APO TOON METRIOON EP' AMECHANON
　　ALGOS AEI STENACHOUSA DIOLLUSAI
　　EN HOIS ANALUSIS ESTIN OUDEMIA KAKOON
　　TI MOI TOON DUSPHOROON EPHIEI
　　nothing to be DONE AMEXANON about it
185　why do you want to make it all the harder?

ELEKTRA

　　It wd/ be childish just to forget him,
　　I'd be a ninny. Carried off that way
　　　　　　　a ITUN aien Itun.
　　NEPIOS HOS TOON OIKTROOS
190　OICHOMENOON GONEOON EPILATHETAI
　　ALL' EME G' HA STONOESS' ARAREN PHRENAS
　　HA ITUN AIEN ITUN OLOPHURETAI
　　ORNIS ATUDZOMENA DIOS ANGELOS
　　IOO PANTLAMOON NIOBA SE D' EGOOGE NEMOO
　　　　THEON

job,]/ **174 TMS** you destroy yourself with too much of it; **FC** [wear yourself out]/ **177 TMS** ALLA OUTOI 7 lines/ all ou toi gar ex Aida/ **184f TMS** (Xo/ trying to get idea into what they consider hysteric female.)/ **185 TMS** (I'd like to know?); dem' if I see why/ **189 TMS** (then whole strophe from NEPIOS)/ **205 TMS** two lines,

195   HAT' EN TAPHOOI PETRAIOOI
       AIEI DAKRUEIS
       I think my mind groans as the sound of Itys
       lamenting, terrified,
       bringing the news from Zeus
200   Niobe weeping in a stone tomb
       has a better portion from heaven
       weeping forever.
       AT EN TAPHO PETRAIOO
       AIEI DAKRUEIS.

CHORUS

205   OUTOI SOI MOUNAI TEKNON
       ACHOS EPHANE BROTOON
       Not only you, dear,
       everyman alive's got his load
       PROS HO TI SU TOON ENDON EI PERISSA
210   HOIS HOMOTHEN EI KAI GONAI XUNAIMOS
       HOIA CHRUSOTHEMIS DZOOEI KAI IPHIANASSA
       poor Chrysothemis, Iphianassa
       KRUPTAI T' ACHEOON EN HEBAI
       and yr/ boy brother
215   in exile
       god send 'un back to Mycenae
       OLBIOS HON HA KLEINA
       GA POTE MUKENAIOON
       DEXETAI EUPATRIDAN DIOS EUPHRONI
220   BEMATI MOLONTA TANDE GAN ORESTAN

       (English echo)

       till Orestes come to the t h r o n e

---

gk/ **209 TMS** gk/ to Iphianassa/ **231 TMS** KRUPTA . . . . heba/ **216 TMS** rest of
strophe to end/ **220f TMS** eng/ echo./ **230 TMS** snare *deleted*; Luce lowest level of

ELEKTRA

whom I keep on expecting,
childless, wretched,
225   unwed, in a dither of fear
muddly with tears,
one thing after another, unending, and always worse;
and he's forgotten all
that's ever happened to him or been told him
230   every message I get is a cheat
always he wants to come
and never shows up

CHORUS (chorus moving/ clear cut position: pause/ move)

THARSEI MOI THARSEI TEKNON
235   ETI MEGAS OURANOOI
ZEUS HOS EPHORAI PANTA KAI KRATUNEI
HOOI TON HUPERALGE CHOLON NEMOUSA
METH' HOIS ECHTHAIREIS HUPERACHTHEO MET'
      EPILATHOU
CHRONOS GAR EUMARES THEOS
240   OUTE GAR HO TAN KRISAN
BOUNOMON ECHOON AKTAN
PAIS AGAMEMNONIDAS APERITROPOS
OUTH' HO PARA TON ACHERONTA THEOS ANASSOON

ELEKTRA

Hopeless and there's no help,
245   wasted already, gone by in despair
no going back on that
fatherless

lousery; the fatted slugs of yr liary/ **232 TMS** aXioOO/ choose; **FC** but never shows up; GREEK/ **233ff TMS** STROPHE THARSEI MOI; **FC** [sung]/ **244ff FC** gone, gone so much,/ hopeless and no redress/ gainst time that's gone, nothing to ward that off/ fatherless, loverless, without stand-bye/ a worthless waif,/ roofed where my father wed;/ in a shapeless sack,/ to feed from vacant board *deleted*; [To] stand around at [the empty tables]/ [&° to be] fed on [their] trash./ **252ff FC** [O.K. to repeat if

loverless
housed neath my father's bed
250   kenneled and fed on trash
in a shapeless sack.

CHORUS *(chorus moving/ pause/ move)*

THARSEI MOI etc. . . . . . ANASSOON.

ELEKTRA

gone, gone so much,
255   hopeless and no redress
gainst time that's gone, nothing to ward that off
fatherless, loverless, without stand-bye
a worthless waif,
roofed where my father wed;
260   in a shapeless sack,
to stand around the empty tables
and to be fed on their trash.

CHORUS

She'd a gloomy voice when he came;
and a gloomy sound when the brass axe hit him,
265   on the couch there in his dining-room.
A twisty idea
and a letch that killed him,
one vehemence led to another
procreating the form
270   whether god or man did it.

ELEKTRA

That was the vilest of all days
and that night at dinner was worse,

sung.]/ **259 TMS** state/plate/ **261 TMS** to feed from vacant board; stand around
at/ **262 TMS** fed on trash./ **263ff FC** [spoken]/ **271 TMS** (hated); **FC** (hated)
deleted/ **272 TMS** and that night's dinner the worst/ **273f TMS** horrible weight of

beyond speakable language,
horrible
275   I saw my father killed by the pair of 'em,
and insulted.
Bitched my life, that did, that betrayal.
Zeus avenger, don't let 'em enjoy it unpunished,
make it hurt. Them in their luxury! Agh!

CHORUS

280   Hush. Stop sounding off or talk sense,
Quit piling troubles one on top of the other
always making a row with that grouch of yours
Dont take the discussable to the powerful

only give 'em a handle.

285   *ELEKTRA (starts as if muttering)*

DEINOIS ENANKASTHEN
It's too horrible, I cant keep it in
I know you mean well, it's no use.
Go away and leave me alone,
290   let me have my cry out.

CHORUS

But, dearie, you only make it all worse,
I'm talkin' to you like a mother,
                 you can trust me

---

that unspeakable dinner/ **275 TMS** watched himself being killed impiously by the double hand; **FC** watched himself being killed/ **282 TMS** by your temper/ **283 TMS** go to the powerful with the discussable/ **283f TMS** aei PSuXa POL . . . to end. PLATHEIN; **FC** aei/ psuxa polemous ta de tois dunatois/ ouk erista plathein *deleted*/ **285 TMS** greek; **FC** [denois enankasthen]/ **292 TMS** I'm talkin to you like a mother?/ **294 TMS** But the worst goes beyond all limit; is there any comparative

ELEKTRA

295

300

305

Is there any limit to the nature of misery?
Is there anything pretty about neglecting the dead?
Has that idea cropped up anywhere among men?
If so I dont want their respect
and if I come near to getting any good from it
may I not live tranquil among 'em
by smothering my keening for the shame of this house.
For if the dead lie down—earth and then—nothing,
wretched
and there be no death for a death
shame wd go wrack,
all duty wd end & be nothing

CHORUS

I rushed out here for your sake as well as mine
if you dont like what I say, have it yr/ own way
we'll stick by you.

ELEKTRA

310

I'm sorry, I oughtn't to let 'em get me down,
but I am driven.

degree (measure) inherent in the worst; worst is not comparative; Limit, is there any limit to what misery I have to endure/ Is there any LIMIT to misery/ inherent in, to the nature of *deleted*/ **295 TMS** shall the dead have no honour, how come?; how neglect decency to dead; tell me there's anything pretty about neglecting the dead/ **296 TMS** has that idea sprouted anywhere among men; cropped up anywhere in any man; has that cropped up in any human/ any one of (all) men; in any man of any race?/ **297 TMS** may I not be honoured among them/ **298 TMS** and if I get any profit out of 'em; nor enjoy profit from them if it come to me./ **299 TMS** may I not enjoy it; may it make me uneasy; may it make me uneasy to be among 'em **300 TMS** or if I end *deleted* [by] my keening for the shame of this house; the not hon-ouring wings of my keening; by smothering; hold in, hold down/ **301 TMS** for if this one (of the dead) lie down, earth and then nowt; **FC** [nothing]/ **302 TMS** lie wretched; **FC** lie *deleted*/ **303 TMS** no return justice given (given right)/ **304 TMS** shame will go wrack; will not all shame for the death rights go wrack./ to wrack ruin; if shame goes, all piety for the dead goes with it/ awe for the dead; **FC** shame will go wrack [wd/]/ **305 FC** [all duty wd/ end & be nothing]/ **309 TMS** forgive

They've got the power, all I can do is yammer
and make too much noise.
I'm ashamed of this clatter.
How cd/ any decently brought up girl
315   see that done to her father, and act any different?
I see it day and night getting thicker, not dying down,
and my own mother the most loathsome of all
and I have to live in the same house with
the people who murdered my father
320   and have 'em pushing me round
WHACK, take it, WHACK, leave it,
always the same, which ever way they've hexed it.
How do you think I pass my time, anyhow?
when I see Aegisthus sitting there
325   in my father's chairs
even wearing his clothes
pouring libations
right by where he killed him
then havin' mother right there in the same bed
330   just to show off, a whore, a mother? call it
a concubine
she's got so used to the dirty slob,
no longer scared of the curse
celebrates with a dance once a month
335   with a whole sheep for "his" dinner.
Joke that is.
                but it gets me down all the same.
And I go moulder in an attic
and blubber over "Agamemnon's bean-O," yes
340   they call it by old pop's name.

my making all this fuss; me for making/ **310 TMS** I am druv to it; **FC** [BUT] druv
to it *deleted* [driven]/ **311 TMS** all I can do is to yammer/ **312 TMS** Excuse it; **FC**
Excuse it *deleted*/ **314 TMS** Could anybody who's been decently brought up/ **315
TMS** do any different?; act any other how?/ **316 TMS** (I see it)/ **321 TMS** whack/
take it, whack, leave it; get going, stop it; they determine what I am told to do, and
what I get done; what I am started on/ what I get for it; WHACK, get on with it;
WHACK, thats what you get/ **322 TMS** which ever way they have hexed it/ **332
TMS** defiler/ **333 TMS** gods *deleted*/ **335 TMS** sheepsac/ **338 TMS** back in my

can't even have my cry out in peace
with that old big-talk bawling me out:
"You the only slut ever lost a father,
nobody else has any troubles,
345   go rot and keep on yowling in hell."
That's how she goes on
EXCEPT when someone says Orestes is comin'
then she gets scared and blows her top proper
goes shoutin' frantic:
350   "You got him away, it's all your fault,
you cheated me out of Orestes, you sneak,
mark my word,
you'll get your come-uppence."
That's her bark, and her ponce sicks her on,
355   marvelous,
of all the dastardly yellow pests,
fightin' from under her skirts
and me rotting away, waiting here for Orestes
to put a stop to it all.
360   and he's worn out all hope, by waiting,
dither and dally,
yes, my dears, a nice place for moderation and decency
and with all this rot I've gone rotten.

CHORUS

Is Aegisthus here, while you're talkin'?

ELEKTRA

365   Naturally NOT. Think I could get out, with him in?

CHORUS

Well then, I can say what I think.

---

room kata stegas [wh is attic]/ **341 TMS** can even *etc.*/ **346 TMS** (bubbles over);
FC That's how she goes on, bubbles over/ **354 TMS** with her bed-boy sicking her to
it; beside her/ **356 TMS** of all the yellow (cowards)/ **357 TMS** behind *deleted*/ **370
TMS** a man's inclined to go slow on a big job/ **372f TMS** Hang on, he wont let you

ELEKTRA

He's out, you can say what you like.

CHORUS

Well about yr/ brother, is he coming or not?

ELEKTRA

Sez he will an' he dont.

CHORUS

370   A man's likely to take his time on a big job.

ELEKTRA

If I'd gone slow, he wdn't be there to take it.

CHORUS

Hang on, he was born honest,
he wont let you down, cares too much

ELEKTRA

If I didn't think that, I'd be dead.

CHORUS

375   Sshh, here comes yr/ sister.
I see she's carrying . . . eh. . . . offerings,
like for DOWN THERE *(points downward)* all very proper.

CHRYSOTHEMIS *(tone of thorough weariness, and
discouragement)*

Oh Dear, are you out here again, sounding off,

down./ cares too much; wont let his friends down; he's too straight/ to let his friends
down/ **374 TMS** I'd die; **FC** (I wouldn't have lived as long as I have) *deleted/* **377
TMS** [(echo) tois katoo nomidzetai]; **FC** (points) [downward]/ **379 TMS** sounding

380   never learn, makes it worse
       let out every fool feeling you got in yr/ gizzard.
       I dont like the mess any better than you do,
       If I could get hold of the power
       I'd show 'em what I think,
385   but for the present I'm going to let down my sail
       pipe down, and not think I'm hurting 'em when I'm not.
       and I advise you to do the same
       What I say to 'em isn't so, and what you think is,
       but I've got to obey in order to keep my freedom of action.

       ELEKTRA

390   It's just awful the way you take her part
       and forget him.
       YOU didn't think of any of that
       it's just what she told you.
       you can do one of two things: be honest and speak out,
395   or play dumb and forget your friends
       You just said if you had the power
       you'd show how you hate 'em
       but when I'm all out to do right by my father,
       will you come in on it? No. You try to put me off it.

yr voice/ **380 TMS** in all this time/ **381 TMS** not to let out every crazy impulse/ useless, fury; not gratify follies of vain rage./ grat/ impulse; give way to/ fool useless,/ **382 FC** I don't like it any better than you do/ **383f TMS** but if I cd/ see how do anything about it; I'd turn loose if cd/ do any good.; If I cd/ get hold of the levers, sieze power/ I'd show 'em; If I cd/ get hold of the power, the levers,/ I'd show 'em. (what I think); **FC** the levers *deleted*/ **385 TMS** for the present I'm going to keep in my sail/ **386 TMS** suborn/ enter secretly; **FC** and not think I'm harming 'em when I'm not/ **388 FC** (just the same I know you're right and)/ what I say isn't so, and what you think is,/ **392 TMS** You haven't thought of any that [*sic*]/ **394 TMS** you can do one of two things: play dumb/ or forget your friends; play dumb. or play clever and forget your own; got a low mind,/ or think it clever to forget those you care for?? the people you like/ **396f TMS** If you had the power you show you hate 'em/ you say/ **398f TMS** but you wont help me get back on 'em/ I'm out to avenge our father/ you not only wont help, you try to persuade me out it [*sic*]; but when I'm all out to honor my father/ you wont help, no, you try to put me off it/ **401 TMS**

*(pause: very clearly enunciated: different tempo: pausing
between each word)*

Need we add cowardice to all the rest of this filth?

Tell me, or lemme tell you what good it cd/ do me
to stop objecting out loud
I'm not dead yet, it's a dirty life
405   but my own.
It annoys 'em. That honours the dead,
if the dead get any joy out of *that*.
You say you hate 'em, but
you play ball with our father's assassins
410   Well I wdn't knuckle under, not for one minute
nor for all this stuff they have given you

*(takes hold of Chrysothemis' bangles or bracelet, or
whatever ornament, or fine dress—some smallish
ornament, in contrast to Klytemnestra's overload)*

that you swank about in.
415   Have yr/ big dinners, comforts
and everything easy,
     your lie-down flow-about life.
If I don't eat, I don't make myself spew with disgust.
Keep my self-respect anyhow
420   I wouldn't want to have a sense of honour like yours
nor wd/ you if you understood it
you're even called by your mother's name
when you cd/ use father's
          and he was some good
425   best of the lot of 'em.
It dont look nice.
most people wd. say you are going back
on yr/ dead father, and the people you care for.

Dont add cowardice to all the rest of this filth/ **404 TMS** I aint dead yet/ **407 TMS** if the dead like it; if the dead get any pleasure out of that *deleted*; **FC** (THAT) *deleted*/ **417 TMS** lie-down flow-about life; **FC** [your]/ **418 TMS** sick *deleted* with disgust; (Only food not to annoy myself)/ **420 TMS** I wdn't swap for your kind of a sense of honour/ **422 TMS** you even carry your mother's name *deleted*/ **430 TMS** you've

CHORUS

430
For the gods' sake, keep your tempers,
there's something to be said on both sides
if either of you cd/ learn from the other.

CHRYSOTHEMIS

Oh, I'm used to the way she goes on.
I wouldn't have come here now, but she's in worse
    danger,
in fact they want to stop her howls once and for all.

ELEKTRA

435
Well what can be worse? If you'll tell me
anything worse, I'll shut up.

CHRYSOTHEMIS

All I know is that if you dont quit bawling
they'll shut you up where you'll never see daylight
in some black jail outside the country,
440
do stop to think, and dont blame me
when it's too late.

ELEKTRA

So that's what they're up to.

CHRYSOTHEMIS

As soon as Aegisthus gets back

ELEKTRA

The sooner the better

CHRYSOTHEMIS

445   So he can?
You're off yr/ poor head. What for?

ELEKTRA

To get away from the lot of you
as far as possible

CHRYSOTHEMIS

But at least you're alive here?

ELEKTRA

450   A beautiful life, something for me to admire

CHRYSOTHEMIS

Might have been if you'd learned to adjust yourself

ELEKTRA

Don't educate me up to double crossing my friends.

CHRYSOTHEMIS

I'm only telling you to bend and not break
when you come up against power.

ELEKTRA

455   Slobber over 'em. Not my way.

CHRYSOTHEMIS

It's perfectly respectable not to fail
out of sheer stupidity.

---

far as possible)/ **455 TMS** (You just dont get me; **FC** *deleted*/ **458 TMS** All right

ELEKTRA

All right I'll fail, for my father's honour
if it's so ordered.

CHRYSOTHEMIS

460   I am sure he'd excuse one.

ELEKTRA

You commend everything nasty.

CHRYSOTHEMIS

Well I suppose you wont listen to anything I say
let alone agree with it.

ELEKTRA

Probably NOT. Not yet such a zero.

CHRYSOTHEMIS

465   Well, I'll be moving along.

*ELEKTRA (noticing the offerings for the first time, having
been up to now absorbed in her own fury)*

Goin' far?
What you carrying THAT for,
470   all roasted?

CHRYSOTHEMIS

Mother told me to go water the grave.

ELEKTRA

What !! and nobody whom she hates worse?

I'll fall/ **460 TMS** I know he'd excuse one/ **464 TMS** Not yet such a cipher; (empty
to that degree); **FC** [zero]/ **469 TMS** Uh'uh. what you carrying THAT for; **FC** Uh'uh

CHRYSOTHEMIS

You mean the one she murdered

ELEKTRA

Where did she get THAT fancy?

CHRYSOTHEMIS

475   Had a nightmare, I think, and it scared her.

ELEKTRA

Gods help us. Whatever next!

CHRYSOTHEMIS

That's cheered you up, now she's scared.

ELEKTRA

You tell me about that dream, then I'll talk.

CHRYSOTHEMIS

I dont really know much about it.

ELEKTRA

480   Spill it. a little word often counts for a lot,
       down or up

CHRYSOTHEMIS

What they say is that it was like as if dad
stood there right by her, and a second time

---

deleted/ **473 TMS** (the one she finished off)/ **474 TMS** What dear friend put her
up to that?; where did she take that fancy; what she want to do that for; what come
over her; **FC** (Whose idea was it?) *deleted/* **477 TMS** Now she scared/ **478 TMS**
(You tell me what she saw, then I'll talk)/ **480 TMS** (tell what you do know)/ **481**
TMS good or bad; **FC** up or down/ **493 TMS** you listen to me now/ **495 TMS**

in plain daylight. And took hold of his sceptre,
485   the one Aegisthus uses now, and planted it by the altar
and a branch grew right out of it

and spread over all Mycenae.

That's what one of the girls says, who was there
while she was telling it before Helios.
490   That's all I know except that she was so scared
she sent me out. Now listen
you pray to the gods. Dont be a fool
listen to me, before it's too late.

ELEKTRA

Don't put a bit of it on the tomb
495   It's not clean before man or gods that you
plant gifts or carry lustrations
from that hating woman, to dirty his grave.
throw 'em away, bury 'em, hide 'em deep
so long as none of 'em gets near his grave.
500   Let 'em stay and wait for HER till she dies
let her find 'em in hell, when she dies,
a little deposit.
The crust she's got, wanting to put flowers
on the grave of the man she murdered,
505   you think the dead from his grave is goin' to
reach up a lovin' right hand for these ornaments?

Killed him like any damn foreigner,
and wiped 'er bloody 'ands on his 'air,
cut off his hands and feet to keep the

Couldn't be anything worse for our luck; the stuff wd. be all under the curse/ **496
FC** (water) *deleted*/ **497 TMS** to him from that hating woman/ **498 TMS** Scatter
it to the wind, bury it/ **499 TMS** so nothing can defile father's grave; none of it; so
they can't dirty his grave/ **503 TMS** from the beginning of time nothing like it of/
all born bitches; of all born bitches from the beginning of time/ nothing like it/ the
crust of her (wantin' to)/ throw her dirty water onto him/ (after bumping him off)/
507ff TMS killed him like any low foreigner,/ cut off his hands and feet to keep the/
ghost from walkin and grabbin her/ and wiped off the blood on his hair/ **511f TMS**

510   ghost from walkin and grabbin her.
       But dont YOU think of carrying that
       stuff to purge her of murder.
       Chuck it away.
       Cut off the tip of one of yr/ curls
515   and this hank of mine

       (jerks out a lock of her own (wig) violently)

       and my belt, it's not much,
       just a plain belt without ornaments.
       But kneel and beg him to come up out of the earth
520   to protect us,
       and that young Orestes get the upper hand of his enemies
       and stay alive till he's got 'em under his feet,
       so that we can crown him with something better
       than what we give now

525   I think mebbe he's troubling her dreams
       Anyhow, you do this for me, and for him
       even if he is dead, we still love him.

       CHORUS

       She's on the right track now, dear,
       you do what she says.

       CHRYSOTHEMIS

530   I certainly will, it's what ought to be done
       and no sense in arguing it.
       But keep quiet about it for gods' sake
       if the old screw gets wind of it
       she'll make me pay for the risk.

You aren't thinking of carrying that stuff/ to purge her murder?/ Anyhow, DONT./
515f TMS of me wretched, small but as is/ my unbrushed mop; **FC** *deleted*/ **519**
TMS But kneel and beg him to send up aid from the earth/ against our enemies;
help; protecting; protector/ **531 TMS, FC** and no sense discussing it/ **532 TMS** for
the gods' sake/ **533 TMS** dont let mother get wind of it; my our [the] usuress; [our
usuress]/ **534 TMS** if she does she'll make me pay extra for the risk; wont go easy

CHORUS

535   You can say that I never guess right
       a fool born without second sight,
       that my head was never screwed tight
       But if Justice don't win just this once
       I'm a dunce
540   and before a great time has gone by
       My heart's risin now
       and my dreams are breathin deep
       with a free and airy sound :
       the greek king wont forget you
545   but he'll be comin yet
       and the double headed axe
       be payin back the smacks

       and the bloody blood be flowin' once again.

       And Vengeance will come out
550   from her hiding bush no doubt
       she will come with brazen tread
       to their adulterous bed
       to wipe out all the stain
       as they wrestle there unwed;
555   ever with lock and sign

on anyone *deleted*/ **535ff TMS** You can say dat I nivver guess right, a fool born widout second sight/ that my head was never screwed tight/ but if Justice dont once/ show the old swine for a dunce; win this case, I'm a dunce/ and before a gt/ toime has gone bye; its a long time indeed, to sprout up from its seed; it wont be long now/ Sure there music in me dream,/ fer to rouse me, it seems/ my spirits are now risin,/ and in dreams most surprisin,/ the chief of all the greek, will becomin in 3 weeks/ the double headed axe, will be payin back the smacks; attacks/ The greek king wont forget, for sure/ and he'll be comin yet/ my hearts a risin now; courage inside/ **549ff TMS, FC** wid the sound of brazen shoes; with a rush of brazen shoes/ of the royal blood they shed/ to their unhallowed bed./ wipe out all the stain from their unholy bed/ for all the blood they shed/ under an evil sign/ fate is stronger than man, blacker darker than man/ never in time nor place/ cometh a monstrous sign/ to the blameless/ to doer and mate *deleted*; unblamed draws near the portent *deleted*; but foretells/ and the divinations of men/ are not in awful dreamings nor in oracles/ if that phantasm of the night/ does not well/ destroy/ making a good smash./ if it dont damn well smash 'em./ that night-sight [?] *these preliminary drafts deleted*/ **582 FC** [spo-

ill doer and ill do's mate
shall never dodge out of fate
ill done hath ill do won
black ends that which black began
560   fate shall out run any man
Nothing foretells tomorrow to man
neither horrors in dreams nor in oracles
ef thet night-sight dont damn well smash 'em.

(*SING the GREEK*)

570   OO PELOPOS HA PROSTHEN
POLUPONOS HIPPEIA
HOOS EMOLES AIANES
TADE GA
EUTE GAR HO PONTISTHEIS
575   MURTILOS EKOIMATHE
PANCHRUSEOON DIPHROON
DUSTANOIS AIKIAIS
PRORRIDZOS EKRIPHTHEIS
OU TI POO
580   ELEIPEN EK TOUD' OIKOI
POLUPONOS AIKIA

(*Chorus Leader speaks*)

For Myrtil's curse
when he was drowned after that crooked horse-race
585   chucked out of his gilded car into the sea

and the curse has continued
on the house of Pelops
rotting the earth.

KLYTEMNESTRA (*entering*)

590   Out here again making trouble, might have known it,
now Aegisthus' not here,

ken meditative]/ **586 TMS** and the curse, contumely, has continued/ **590 TMS** just
like you/ **594f TMS** (however); you've told a lot of people; you've let off a lot to a

he keeps you from making dirt on your friends' doorstep.
he's away and you pay no attention to me
you've shot off a lot of brash talk
595   to a lot of people
a lot more than was so
about how forward I am, how unjust
insulting you and your gang

Nobody ever insulted me? Eh??
600   Bad, eh?
well I've heard 'em from you often enough
just as bad.
Your father, eh? always that, never different
that's your excuse
605   I killed him,
yes, me, and a good job, dont I know it,
'ave I ever denied it?
with Justice on my side, I wasn't alone
as you'll have to admit if you think straight

610   This "father" you're always crying about
was the only one of the greeks who wd/ stand for
sacrificing your own sister to the gods,
he didn't have as much trouble in makin' her as I had
he put her in, I got her out
615   Well, who did he sacrifice her FOR?
you tell me, for whom an' for what?
The greeks. You say for the greeks?
which of two greeks was it?
it wasn't up to them to kill my girl
620   and if he killed her for his brother
hadn't I got any rights?
Hadn't Menelaus two children of his own
wasn't it up to them to die, if it was

lot of people/ **597 TMS** that I am insolent and unjust; a great deal about my bein'
brash and unjust/ **598 TMS** and the insults I heap on you and yours/ **606 TMS** I
did, and a good job too *deleted*; **FC** it was *deleted*/ **609 TMS** (one has to defend
(help) oneself; necessity defends itself; does it need defending?; if you happened to
be intelligent, so disposed/ **610 TMS** blabbering over *deleted*/ **620 TMS** (Melelaus);

their father and mother who were cause of the sailing.
625   Did Hell want mine more than hers?
or had the rotter less paternal affection
than Menelaus?
Signs of a gutless and dirty father? I say
they are, even if we split on it.

630   And it's what your dead sister wd/ say if she cd/ manage a
voice
I'm not peeved about what I've done
and if you want to sling abuse
try slinging it at somebody else in the family
get on the right track, put the blame where it belongs.

635   *ELEKTRA (calm)*

Well this time you can't say I started it.
but if you'll let me, I'll give you the rights of it
about my father and sister

KLYTEMNESTRA

Of course I'll let you, and if you
640   had always used that tone of voice
no one wd/ have objected to listening.

ELEKTRA

All right, you admit you killed him,
can anyone say anything worse?

FC brother Menelaus/ **621 TMS** weren't there any rites due to me; **FC** [hadn't I got
any rights?]/ **622 TMS** he got *deleted*/ **624 TMS** wasn't it their father and mother,/
that all the sailing was being done for./ **625 TMS** Hell thirsting for my children
rather than hers; to feast on; to fill up on; to the full on; **FC** (have more appetite) for
my children than hers *deleted*/ **626 TMS** skipped the rotter and got into M/ **629
TMS** even if we hold opposite views on the matter/ **630 TMS** handle her voice/
633f TMS keep yr/ head and blame someone else in the family *deleted*; think I'm on
the wrong track; if I seem to think evily; get on the right one, and blame somebody
nearer to you; **FC** and *deleted* (put the blame where it belongs)/ **637 TMS** but if it is
permitted, I'll put the facts/ **638 TMS** about dad and my sister/ **639 TMS** you're

legally or illegally?
645   Well justice didn't come into it.
it was your letch for that bounder you're living with.
Go ask Artemis and her dogs why she
shut up the winds in Aulis
all of them, for what vengeance.
650   and as she wont tell you, I will:
He was hunting away thru her forest
and not only started a spotted buck with 8 points
but made smutty jokes about it, it was
a kill
655   not according to hunting rites.
And Artemis didn't like it
she held up the Achaeans
to make my father pay
for the buck with his own daughter.
660   that's why and how she was killed.
she went to the altar smokes
a sacrifice,
the troops couldn't get either home or to Ilion
no other way out.
665   He did it against his own nature
not in favour of Menelaus.
But even if he had done it for Menelaus, to take it your
    way,
ought you to have killed him?
What law was that?
670   You'd better be careful setting up that sort of law

allowed; **FC** [I'll let you]/   **656 TMS** was badly enraged; and it put Artemis in such
a great rage/   **657 TMS** that she held up (fell upon) the Achaeans; was so enraged
that she held up the Achaeans/   **658 TMS** life for life *deleted*/   **659 TMS** pay for the
beast brute with his own daughter; sacrifice his own *deleted* daughter to pay for the
animal; paid for the buck with his daughter/   **660 TMS** that was *deleted* her sacrifice, that was the how of it./   **665 TMS** resisting under gt/ constraint; but suffering
and resisting/ in more ways than one; almost without choice; against being, against
his own nature??/   **667 TMS** or if, now take it your way; pull it out your way/ he did
it to help Menelaus,/ and that he was due to die for it/   **668 TMS** were you the person
to kill him. What law,/   **669 TMS** what law of any race/   **670 TMS** you be careful/

for the rest of the world, you'll get into trouble
and wish you hadn't.
for if blood for blood makes justice,
you'll be the first to go.
675   And what you say is all sophistry anyhow,
fake,
say what you like, you get into bed with the murderer
and breed to put out the true heirs,
expect me to like it?
680   Call that avenging a daughter? If that's your excuse?
a dirty job to marry an enemy
for the sake of a daughter?
And nobody aint allowed to warn you
without your puttin up a squawk about slandering mama.
685   Slave-driver more than a mother I'd call you
and a rotten life I have with you and your fellow-feeder
put all the low jobs onto me

And poor Orestes who got away by the skin of his teeth
wearing away out of luck
690   You always accuse me of saving him
to come back and clean up the dirt
and you know damn well I would have too, if I could.
So if I'm a dirty scold, impudent,
completely impertinent,
695   looks like it runs in the family,
from your side at least.

671f TMS (set trouble and repentence [*sic*] to self/ **673f TMS** you are; if its death for death, it's you first,/ if that's justice/ **675 TMS** But look, is all your talk sophistry; **FC** [& what you say is all sophistry anyhow,]/ **676 FC** fake, a mere sophistry *deleted*/ **681f TMS** a dirty job to marry an enemy to do that./ for a daughter/ not pretty at all; marry across a blood-feud for the sake of a daughter?/ a vengeance? a dirty job; not pretty to/ **683 TMS** and nobody cant (go out to) warn you/ **684 TMS** (dirty-mouth)/ **685 TMS** (to us, I'd say)/ **687 FC** you're always putting *deleted*/ **689 TMS** (in misery); **FC** in misery/ **690 TMS** You often/ **691 TMS** clean off your dirt; **FC** (you've done here) *deleted*/ **692 TMS** so I did, if only he could; as you'll damn well find out (and if I did??); you got it (get it)/ you've got it./ (I SHOULD worry); Wouldn't I have, if only he could/ **695 TMS** If I am; If I'm good at it, the dirt runs in the family; the trade technique runs/ **696 TMS, FC** not likely to disgrace your

CHORUS

Gheez, she's a-goin' it fierce,
right or not she dont care a hang.

KLYTEMNESTRA

700   Why should I bother what she thinks
spittin' out at her mother that way, at her age,
Bi god there's nothing she'd stop at,
no sign of shame

ELEKTRA *(suddenly perfectly calm)*

Well now I think I have got a sense of shame
705   I distinguish between suitable conduct
and what I am driven to by yr/ hate and yr/ devilments.
dirty workers teach dirty work.

KLYTEMNESTRA

You beastly whelp, it's what I've said
and NOT done, that makes you talk a great deal too
        much.

ELEKTRA

710   Now you're talkin',
you did the job, not me,
and things done get names
                    nomina sunt consequentia rerum

KLYTEMNESTRA

By the Virgin you'll pay for this
when Aegisthus gets home.

temperament *deleted*/   **698 TMS** what (she says) she's saying/ not stopping to think;
(no sign of thought)/   **702 TMS** (sense)/   **705 TMS** suitable to a young lady;/   **708f
TMS** its my talking and/ not taking action that makes you talk *deleted*; and a lot I
haven't done that makes you talk too much/   **710 TMS** Now you're talkin' for both
of us, not me,/   **714 TMS** By Goddess; (cheek)/   **716 TMS** tell(s)/   **717 TMS** (haven't

ELEKTRA

715   Nice nature comin' out, ain't it?
       temperamental, tells me to say what I like
       and hasn't got brains enough to hear it.

KLYTEMNESTRA

       You'd even spoil the sacrifice, shouting
       now I've let you get it all out.

720   *ELEKTRA (coldly)*
       Go along, yes, DO sacrifice, please
       and dont say my noise is jinxing you,
       I wont say anything more.

KLYTEMNESTRA (to maid)

725   Here, you, pick up all this fruit and incense,
       so I can pray and get rid of these worries

       (sotto voce)

       Hear me Apollo, Patron,
       keep down this scandal
730   don't answer so these spies can get it
       (I am not speaking this among friends)
       cant spill it all out with her here
       ready to yatter
       and spread mean silly nonsense all thru the town
735   envious little bitch
       But do hear me, let me explain
       this ghost in the shifty vision of a dream
       O Apollo Lykeios, if it's lucky let the luck come to me
       and if it's evil, let it fall on my enemies,
740   if anybody's trying to cheat me out of my money
       don't let 'em.

---

got)/ **726 TMS** so I can get *deleted* the king off me mind; that are *deleted* scarin'
me/ **728 TMS** (guardian)/ **733 TMS** spread *deleted*; **FC** she is ready to yatter/ **734**
TMS dirty nonsense *deleted*/ **735 TMS** (envious little bitch)/ **746 TMS** full of spite

Let me run the house of Atreides as long as I live
and keep hold of the sceptre. Preserve me
to live comfortably with these friends,
745   and with children who like me
and who aren't gone bitter with spite and gloom
O Phoibos Lyceios hear me, with favour
give to us all that we ask,
and you know all the rest I dont say
750   for the sons of God see all that there is.

TUTOR

I'm a stranger in these parts, can
any of you kind ladies tell me
ef that's Milord Aegisthus's palace?

CHORUS

Yes, stranger, you've hit it, bullseye.

TUTOR

755   Would I be right in sayin that woman there is the queen?
She looks it.

CHORUS

She's it

TUTOR

Gruss Gott, your Highness, I've got good
news for you and Aegisthus, Come from a friend of his.

KLYTEMNESTRA

760   That's nice.
(dropping voice) wonder who the deuce that can be.

---

deleted; (ill will)/   **752 TMS** (kind)/   **766 TMS** (I'm finished)/   **771 TMS** to PAID/

TUTOR

Phanoteus, of Phocia. It's a serious matter.

KLYTEMNESTRA

Well, what is it? go on, stranger
must be good if it comes from him.

TUTOR

765   Orestes is dead. That's the short of it.

ELEKTRA

Oooh, that's the end. I'm finished.

KLYTEMNESTRA

What, what, don't bother with her.

TUTOR

He's dead. Orestes, finish! na poo.

ELEKTRA

Ruin, ruin, I can't go on.

KLYTEMNESTRA

770   (*to Elektra*) Mind your own business.
Now, stranger, tell me about it,
how did it happen?

TUTOR

That's what I'm here for. He went up for the big Delphic
        proize
that's the biggest greek games
775   and when he heard the herald yellin' out for the first race

773 **FC** prize/   778 **TMS** ub; **FC** [v]/   782 **TMS** umPIREs/   786 **TMS** gods' *deleted*/

the foot race, he came out shining
admired of all beholders
an' he got the proize uv the first race
I never see a man like him, from start to finish
780   the crown he had for the victory
I'm only tellin' the part of it.
He took all the foive proizes, you could hear the umpires
tellin' it: Agamemnon's son, young Orestes.
Win for Argos. Old general's son licked the lot of 'em.

785   (*change tone, and shaking head*)

There's no lickin' the god's bad temper
An' the next day toward sundown
he entered, there were all of the charioteers,
Sparta, Achaia, and two boys from Libya:
790   drivers, and one team of thessalian mares;
an Aeolian, young chestnut fillies, and another from
      Megara.
A white Aneian, and the Athenian, number nine,
the city the gods put up, and last and tenth the Beotian.
And the umpires ranged 'em up as the lot fell
795   and they sounded off with the brazen horn
shakin' the reins and a-lickin' the horrses
and a yellin' till you couldn't hear over the plain
and the track wuz narrow, the lot of 'em drivin' togedder
and a-lammin' the horses, each one tryin' to git out of
800   the bunches
and the wheels a-rollin', and the horses a-snortin'
and their sweat spattered over the cars,
and their breath steamin' on the droivers in front of 'em
and Orestes come round at the turn, at the turns
805   all of 'em, shavin' the pillars
loosin' the off horse and pullin' in on the nigh,
And the Anenian's bolted between the sixth and the 7th
      round
and foul'd the Barcaen's, and they all piled up then
the lot of 'em.

789 TMS Spartha/   **803 TMS** in from of [*sic*]/   **838 FC** GENOS/   **840 TMS** (?? all

810   except the Athenian
                         who slowed up
             and then Orestes
                         pulled in on his team
             nothin' left but the two of 'em
815   all RIGHT, till the very last turn, when his
             axle-tip hit the pillar
                         and busted
             and he got t'rown over the rail
             and caught in the reins of his horses
820   wid the crowd yellin' for pity
             now seein' him bumped on the ground and now lifted
             wid his feet in the air
                         till the other charioteers
             got hold of his horses
825   and found him
                         broke beyond recognition,
             his best friend wouldn't have known him.

             (*pauses*)

             And the Phoceans burnt it then and there on a pyre
830   and the envoys are comin', bringin' what's left in an urn
             to lay his dust in his fatherland.
             It's a sad story, madam, I
             saw it wid me own eyes.
             Never a worse one.

             CHORUS

835   Ah, ah, that's the end of the dynasty
                         TO PAN DE DESPOTAISI TOIS PALAI
             They are blotted out root and branch.
                         HOOS EOIKEN, EPHTHARTAI.

             KLYTEMNESTRA

             Oh god. what, which, I dunno if it's lucky.
840   Terrible, if it's terrible, it's, it's useful anyhow

to the good)/ **841f TMS** its distressing to have to save ones life/ by misfortunes; my

it's a miserable state of things when
nothing but my own sorrows save my own life.

TUTOR

What, lady, am I gettin you down with this news?

KLYTEMNESTRA

That's the worst of being a mother,
845   can't hate a child no matter how badly they treat you.

TUTOR

Seems I came on a useless errand.

KLYTEMNESTRA

No, not useless, if you've got sure proof of his death
born of my life, forgetful of the breasts that suckled him
banished himself to get away from me
850   never seen me since he left the country
accused me of killing his father
and he was threatening
                what awful things he wd/ do
till I cdn't get a night's sleep or a cat nap
855   thinking I was going to die every minute
and now, eh, now I needn't be scared of him any more
nor of that worse little bloodsucker living here with me,
the pest,
now we'll get a day's peace somewhere
860   in spite of her threats.

own troubles/ sorrows/ misfortunes/ **843 TMS** depressing you/ **844f TMS** awful to
be a mother./ worst of being a mother, she cant/ hate her children, no matter what
they do to her; thats the awful thing about being a/ awful to be a mother, cant hate
yr/ children/ no matter how badly they treat you/ **852 TMS, FC** terrible *deleted*/
859 TMS There'll be somewhere to live; Live in peace despite her threats; in peace/
because she wont be threatening; some peace undisturbed by her/ threats, so we can

ELEKTRA

Ooooh, he's dead. and it fits her book
motherly excitement
very pretty

KLYTEMNESTRA

Not for you. I dare say He's better off.

ELEKTRA

865   Holy vengeance—god hear her,
and him not cold in the grave.

KLYTEMNESTRA

Fate HAS heard, and managed it very nicely.

ELEKTRA

Go on, keep it up. You're top dog,
you've hit the jack-pot.

KLYTEMNESTRA

870   You and Orestes can't spoil it now.

ELEKTRA

Spoil it! No, this is *our* finish.

KLYTEMNESTRA (to Tutor)

You'd deserve more than a good fat tip
if you'd make her hush and finish her yatter.

---

live/ **862f TMS** misery; **FC** ?miserly; **TMS** so she's up on the bottle; very pretty?/
871 FC OUR/ **874 TMS** you cd/: (you'd)/ **881 TMS** (makin fun of the dead)/ **886f**

TUTOR

875   Well, m'am, I'll be goin', if everything is in
good shape.

KLYTEMNESTRA

No, no, can't treat a friend's messenger that way.
Come in, do, and let her yowl
out here about her friends' troubles, and hers.

ELEKTRA

880   Looks like she's grief-stricken, weepin an' wailin
about her poor son being wiped out that way?
went out bursting with laughter.
                    poor me
                    OO TALAIN' EGOO
885   not ever
I'll lie down at the gate here
and die here, got no friends anyhow.

(*sinks onto step*)

And if anybody kills me, because he dont like it
any of them inside, be a favour,
got no wish to live anyhow.

CHORUS

God, where the hell are you? Zeus,
Apollo, no light and no lightening,
is there no one to show these things up?

TMS till I just wither (dry up) and die/ shrivvel/   **888 FC** (lies down at the gate)
deleted; [sinks onto step]/   **889 TMS, FC** for it *deleted*/   **890f TMS, FC** that killing
deleted; and an affliction if I live, *deleted*/   **894 TMS** seeing you hide ('em) and pass

ELEKTRA

895 AI AI

CHORUS (gesticulating)

No use in crying.

ELEKTRA

AIH

CHORUS

SHHH.

ELEKTRA

900 you are killing me

CHORUS

what?

ELEKTRA

don't tell me about life after death
that's only another kick when I'm down.
they're dead forever

CHORUS (sings)

OIDA GAR ANAKT' AMPHIAREOON CHRUSODETOIS
HERKESI KRUPHTHENTA GUNAIKOON KAI NUN HUPO
   GAIAS
Nay but King Amphiarion
that died for a golden chain
910 caught in a false wife's net
under the earth reigns yet

the buck./ **898 TMS** ajh/ **904 FC** (they're dead and gone forever)/ **905 FC** (sings

ELEKTRA (disgusted and bored with the song)

Ajhh

CHORUS (singing)

915   He reigns and lords his mind
        PAMPSUCHOS ANASSEI

*ELEKTRA (beginning to cheer up, still dubious, but
singing now and echoing the tone of the Chorus)*

AHI

CHORUS

920   and bodes no good at all
        for her who slew him

ELEKTRA

slain

CHORUS

aye, slain

ELEKTRA

    known, over known,
925   mid grief, an avenger.
    OID' OID' EPHANE GAR MELETOOR
    AMPHI TON EN PENTHEI.
    I have none.
    He was, and is not.
930   HOS GAR ET' EN
    PHROUDOS ANARPASTHEIS
    vanished away, torn from me.

softly? trying to comfort her)/ **917 TMS** singing (echo on tone); (EL/ beginning to
cheer up/ still dubious)/ **922 TMS** He died, no less, *deleted*/ **923 TMS** died *deleted*;
FC (echoing); Ay/ **924 FC** (Greek to go with this); o'er/ **934 TMS** overknow; **FC**

CHORUS

sorrow attains thee, sorrow.

ELEKTRA

known, dont I know, over known,
935   day after day, moon over moon,
overfull, pain over pain
horrors of hate abate not
ever.

CHORUS

our eyes be witness

ELEKTRA

940   then do not deceive me
neither lead me astray

CHORUS

thou say'st?

ELEKTRA

not into emptiness
        where there is no one at *all*

945   *CHORUS (the two "alls" simultaneously)*

all men must die

[known]/ **937 TMS** and hate *deleted*/ **941 TMS** do not mislead me into the noth-
ingness/ void/ **944 TMS** where there is no one; ((no comfort left me/ no hope is left
me/ my race is ended.)); (no king's son/ in hoping, comes to uphold me); **FC** [at all]/

ELEKTRA

but to die so, so clawed in whirling doom
torn in the track, if so that death must come . . . .

CHORUS

mid tortures so
950   whose death was unforeseen

ELEKTRA

How not? and him so far
no hand to lay . . . .

CHORUS (here strong AHI)

AHI

ELEKTRA

955   his mangled limbs
in decent grave,
unwept to meet strange clay.

*CHRYSOTHEMIS (very pretty, blonde, just a shade
plump showing heredity from fat, tubby, shortish mama,
trots in puffing)*

960   Oh dearest . . . . so happy . . . . such news . . .
I'm all out of breath from running. . . . .
your troubles are over

ELEKTRA (voice of complete sceptical weariness)

what? you with a cure-all?

965   *(after a pause, and looking her up and down)*

where did you find what ain't?

947f TMS but dreadful death/ under swift racers/ furrowed by cutting wheels; neath
speeding hooves/ torn by the wheels *deleted* dead doom/ cut by the rival's wheel/ be
torn, and die/ **956 TMS** unwept *deleted*/ **970 TMS** it *deleted*; (your and my)/ **974**

CHRYSOTHEMIS

He's here . . . Orestes is here . . .
I'm tellin you, just as sure as you see me.

ELEKTRA

970   You're CRAZY, poor dear, plumb crazy
don't joke about horrors.

CHRYSOTHEMIS

I'm not, I swear by the hearth-stone
he's come for the two of us.

ELEKTRA (sigh)

975   Oh dear, poor dear, has anyone LIVING
put that nonsense into your head?

CHRYSOTHEMIS

No, but me, ME, what I've seen,
me, with my own eyes, seen.

ELEKTRA

WHAT proof? you poor fool
you're blotto delirious.

CHRYSOTHEMIS

980   For gods' sake wait till I finish telling you,
and then decide whether I'm batty

ELEKTRA

All right, go on, if you like to talk.

FC (ghost?)/ **976 FC** from *deleted*/ **979 TMS** seeing delusions, het up with fever/ hopeless (incurable)/ [(lit) incurable]/ **980 TMS** GOD'S *deleted*; the GODS'; tell *de-*

CHRYSOTHEMIS

It was like this
I was goin' to father's old grave
985   and there was milk newly spashed over it
running down from the top of the mound
and all sorts of wreathes all around it
put there for father
like as if

990   *(Elektra masked, at first not even looking at Chrysothemis*
but boredly into distance, gradually grows attentive.
Slowness in turning of head, as per Noh)

and I was wondering, and looking to see who,
who on earth cd/ —
995   and looking to see if anyone might be coming
and when I saw everything quiet
I sneaked up nearer the mound
and there was a new lock of hair on it
right on the edge
1000   and, oh dear, it came over me while I was looking at it
that Orestes had put it there,
dear Orestes, put it there for a sign
almost as if I had seen him
and I picked it up and burst out crying,
1005   I was so happy,
                it can't be ill omen.
and I'm perfectly sure nobody else cd/ have put it there
who'd have cared? except us,
I didn't put it there, and you didn't
1010   cause you couldn't get out of the house,
SHE wouldn't have, she's not taken that way
and she cdn't have, without being seen.

---

leted/ **984 TMS** (tumble-down)/ **993f TMS** (sic. who cd/, who on earth cd/); **FC** who could deleted/ **995 TMS** watching me *deleted*; **FC** as if someone might be coming/ **997 TMS** tomb *deleted*/ **1002 TMS** dear Orestes, there's nobody like him./ there's be; **FC** *omitted*/ **1009 FC** I didn't and you didn't/ **1013 FC** No, no, no,/

No, NO, my dear, Orestes put that stuff on the grave,
you buck up.
1015   The same devils can't always run things,
ours have been pretty bad,
        But the luck's changing,
happen a really good day might come in

ELEKTRA

Poor thing, you always were soft in the head.

CHRYSOTHEMIS

1020   But aren't you glad?

ELEKTRA

you dont know whether you're on earth, or raving.

CHRYSOTHEMIS

dont I know what I've seen with my own eyes, SEEN.

ELEKTRA

He's dead, and the dead wont help you and he cant.
god help you, poor you.

CHRYSOTHEMIS

1025   Oh, o, O, but who told you.

ELEKTRA

A man who was there and saw it. Killed.

CHRYSOTHEMIS (in tone of complete puzzlement)
Where is he, the man? It's very peculiar.

1014 FC (you can buck up now)/   **1023f TMS** (help thence lost,/ never see him./

ELEKTRA (pointing with thumb over shoulder)

1030   In THERE, and mother's so glad to see him.

CHRYSOTHEMIS

Oh dear . . . but whoever can have put all those wreathes
on the tomb?

ELEKTRA

Somebody must have put 'em there for Orestes.

CHRYSOTHEMIS

O. O, and me running to make you happy
1035   and not knowing we'd only come into more trouble
besides what we had.

ELEKTRA

Well that's how it is. And now you turn to and help me,
at least this much with the load.

CHRYSOTHEMIS

You want me to raise the dead?

ELEKTRA

1040   That's not what I said. At least I wasn't born crazy.

CHRYSOTHEMIS

well what do you want me to do, that I can do?

ELEKTRA

Dont break down, and do what I tell you.

---

literally no improvement??)/ **1039 TMS** (wake? or bind to "load"?) *deleted*/ **1040**
TMS I'm not *deleted*; **FC** I/ **1048 TMS** left *deleted*/ **1049 TMS** they've all gone to

CHRYSOTHEMIS

I'll do anything that can be the least use.

ELEKTRA

You can't do a good job without work.

CHRYSOTHEMIS

1045   I know that. I'll do everything that I can.

ELEKTRA

Well then listen.
I'm going to finish it up.
We got no more friends to stand by us
Hell's grabbed the lot
1050   and left us
you can see that. nobody left but us.
As long as HE was alive I went on
hoping he'd come and put things right about father,
wipe out the murder.
1055   Now he's gone, not there any more,
I rely on you
we've got to kill Aegisthus ourselves.
you're not scared?
It's *our* father was murdered.
1060   we've only got our own hands.
might as well look at it straight.
wont get anywhere sittin still,
what hope is left standing
here you are crying and grousing about being cheated out

hell/ **1051 TMS** nobody but us left/ **1052 TMS** one kept hearing that/ **1053 TMS** kept hoping *deleted*/ **1055 TMS** gone *deleted*/ **1056 TMS** (I rely on you); **FC** I hope you won't hold back *deleted*/ **1061 TMS** (all my cards on the table now./ wd/ be anachronism?) or not?/ **1062f TMS** [(]You'll see its the right thing to do.[)]???; you'll be seen as a right (she) 'un; will you etc.??; will you still go lookin' for the right (course); to what standing (of) hopes will you look; No use in waiting, there's not the faintest hope left, is there?; is there any use in??; **FC** *omitted*/ **1064f TMS** are

1065   of father's fortune, that's that,
        and we're not getting any younger
        Dont think they'll ever let you get married,
        Aegisthus wont let us have children,
        he's too cagey for that,
1070   not to put him out of the running
        But you do what I tell you
        FIRST: you'd be showing respect for your dead father
            down under
        AND for your brother as well
        SECONDLY you could live like a free woman, free born, as
            you were,
1075   for the rest of your life,
        and you'd get a fit man to marry.
        People recognize quality, everybody does.
        You listen to me, and we'd both be respected,
        anybody from here or abroad wd/ say:
1080   there they are, those girls saved the dynasty
        risked their lives doing it
        threw out the crooks, settled the murderers' hash.
        You just got to like 'em
        everybody's got to respect 'em

1085   *(dreamy half-tranced voice merging into greek)*

        we'd have our proper place of honour
        in processions and in assemblies
        on account of our courage

        (sing greek)

you going to get your father's fortune/ that they've cheated you out of?; No use in crying about father's fortune/ that we've been cheated out of; **FC** well here it is: *deleted*; [that's that]/ **1066 TMS** We're not getting younger; and that we're not getting younger/ **1067f TMS** unloved, unmarried. Dont think they'll let you get married; without a man, and unmarried/ unmarried, and without a room of your own/ home of your own/ unbedded, unchambered; **FC** without a man and unmarried so long *deleted*/ **1071 TMS** But if you get wise and/ [(]You[)] do what I tell you *deleted*/ **1072 TMS** (with jesture) [*sic*]; (down below there)/ **1074 TMS** secondly, you'd be livin like a free woman, free born (as you were); be able to CALL yr/ soul your own/ be recognized as Eleuthera); **FC** [could live]/ **1080 TMS** their family *deleted*/ **1082**

1090   IDESTHE TOODE TOO KASIGNETOO PHILOI
        HOO TON PATROOION OIKON EXESOOSATEN
        HOO TOISIN ECHTHROIS EU BEBEKOSIN POTE
        PSUCHES APHEIDESANTE PROUSTETEN PHONOU
        TOUTOO PHILEIN CHRE TOODE CHRE PANTAS SEBEIN
1095   TOOD' EN TH' HEORTAIS EN TE PANDEMOOI POLEI
        TIMAN HAPANTAS HOUNEK' ANDREIAS CHREOON
        we'd have a reputation everywhere
        and it wd/ last even when we are dead.

        Trust me, my dear, and stand by your father,
1100   work with me for your brother, get me out of my misery
        get yourself out of yours,
        and remember this, the free born ought not to
        sink into slavery.

        CHORUS

        Well I guess
1105   lookin forward is about the best ally one cd
        have, if you're talking or listenin'
        to things like this

        CHRYSOTHEMIS

        No, girls, if she weren't on the wrong track
        she'd have had a little caution before she sounded off
1110   and she just hasn't got any.

        (to Elektra)

        where do you look to get the nerve to fight
        or get me into the ranks?
        cant you see you were born a *woman* not a *man*
1115   you haven't got the physical strength

TMS (usurpers)/ **1088 TMS** because of *deleted*/ **1098 TMS** (wd.nt be taken from us, stolen)/ **1099 TMS** (? believe me)/ **1102f TMS** (the high born ??); the well-born ought not to sink into squalor; ought to be ashamed of sinking into squalor; **FC** (noblesse oblige) *deleted*/ **1109 TMS** started *deleted*/ **1120 TMS** (of that sort)/

of these people you're up against.
their gods, their luck is comin' up every day
and ours going out, *not* comin' in at all.

(Chrysothemis repetitive and very patient)

1120   You try to break a man like that?
who cd/ get away with it
& not break;
not make a complete mess of it
Dont make it worse
1125   if anybody heard you talkin this way
you'd get into more trouble.
We wont get OUT of anything that way,
and fine talk's no use if we're dirty dead
Death's not the worst that can happen
1130   but not to be able to die when you want to.
I put it to you, before we're completely wiped out
us two and all of the family
keep your temper, hold in.
I'll keep my mouth shut about what you've said
1135   cause I think it's, all of it, useless.
BUT do hang on to your wits, from now on
dont go up against the people in power.

1122 TMS unharmed; **FC** [& not break]/ **1123** (and not make a total wreck); **FC**
and *deleted*/ **1124 FC** the mess *deleted* [it]; by monkeying with it *deleted*/ **1125**
TMS Now if anyone shd/ hear you talkin' this way; if anybody shd/ hear you taking
[*sic*] this way./ **1126 TMS** make a botch and get into worse trouble;/ **1127f TMS**
And fine talk's no use when you're dirty dead; no use to us, if we're dirty dead; (we
wont get OUT of anything,/ and fine talk's no use if we're dirty dead); be able to use
a fine reputation?????? after a dirty death; [cant use reputation when dead]; **FC** [that
way]/ **1130 TMS** but when to die wanting *deleted*; want to die and not be able/
1133 TMS (hide it, keep it dark)/ **1135 TMS** leads to nothing; dont think it will
get anyone anywhere; wont get you anywhere/ **1136 TMS** BUT do have the sense;
hang onto your wits (prudence); keep yr/ own council; (yr/ mind to yourself)/ **1137**
TMS not to go up against the people in power; not to try force/ violence against those
in authority./ ruling./ in power; when its a question of force, yield to those in "authority"; dont yield to the powerful struggling/ **1143 TMS** (I'll)/ **1145 TMS** if you'd

CHORUS (to Elektra)

You better listen, there's nothing more useful
1140   to a human being than forethought, and a prudent mind.

ELEKTRA

Just as I thought . . . . .
all right, I'll do it alone,
it's got to be done—or have a try at it anyhow.

CHORUS

Ooooh, Lord
1145   I wish you'd taken the chance the day he died!
anything was possible then

ELEKTRA

Not that I didn't want to; I hadn't the sense.

CHRYSOTHEMIS

I wish you still had as much

ELEKTRA

that means you won't help me at all.

CHRYSOTHEMIS

1150   It CAN'T be lucky.

ELEKTRA

Nice mind, no guts!

CHRYSOTHEMIS

I can bear up even under that compliment.

done it *deleted/* **1146 TMS** (anything might have happened then)/ **1150 TMS** (or:

ELEKTRA

You wont have to stand any more.

CHRYSOTHEMIS *(blandly)*

1155   That remains to be seen.

ELEKTRA

Oh get out, you're no use at all.

CHRYSOTHEMIS *(a bit peeved)*

I am so, but you can't see it.
you'll never learn.

ELEKTRA

1160   Go tell it all to mama.

CHRYSOTHEMIS *(explanatory)*

But I don't hate you that way.

ELEKTRA

No, but think how you'd lead me to shame.

CHRYSOTHEMIS

No I would NOT.
1165   I'm only asking you to think forward.

ELEKTRA

and accept YOUR values?

Go about it that way/ it can't be lucky.)/ **1159 FC** *omitted*/ **1163 TMS** You might
as well learn for sure; well you sure wd/ dishonour me./ lead me to shame/ (shame
to me); [no but think how]/ **1165 TMS** It's your honour I'm thinking of *deleted*;
(look where you're going)/ **1166 TMS** tie myself up to your values/ **1168 TMS** you can

CHRYSOTHEMIS

When you get untangled, I'll take to yours,
you can think for us both, then.

ELEKTRA

That's talking, too bad you mean it the wrong way on.

CHRYSOTHEMIS

1170   That's just the trouble with you.

ELEKTRA

What? you mean what I say isn't perfectly true?

CHRYSOTHEMIS

EVEN JUSTICE CAN BE A PEST.

ELEKTRA

Anyhow, I dont want to go by your standards of conduct.
I'd rather die.

CHRYSOTHEMIS

1175   But if you did you'd probably find I'm right.

ELEKTRA

I'm going on, anyhow. You can't scare me.

CHRYSOTHEMIS (very soberly)

You're serious? you wont think it over?

---

think for us both./ **1169 TMS** (Its awful when any one argues so well the wrong
way/ on the wrong side); Go wrong/ astray talking so nicely; in the wrong direction/
all off the track/ **1173 TMS** Anyhow, I dont want YOUR kind of law/ **1175 TMS**

ELEKTRA

Nothing stinks worse than bad advice.

CHRYSOTHEMIS

1180   You just dont understand what I'm saying.

ELEKTRA

I've been thinking this way a long time.

CHRYSOTHEMIS *(resignedly)*

Well, I'll go now.
You can't stand my talk, and I dont think
1185   you're going the right way about it.

ELEKTRA

Yes, go along, but I'll never trail after you
for the urging
It's useless to chase after shadows,

(mezzo voce, as if reflecting)

1190   such a lot of them,
all of them void.

CHRYSOTHEMIS

If you ever aim to teach yourself to think straight,
think about it now. You'll think of what I'm saying.
Too . . . . . late.

CHORUS   *Strophe*

1195   TI TOUS ANOOTHEN PHRONIMOOTATOUS OIOON-

(if you do, you will)/ **1180 TMS** I dont in the least mean what you seem to think (I
do)./ **1181 FC** This isn't something that's just come into my head/ **1184 TMS** (you
cant bear to agree with (anything)/ what I say)/ **1185 TMS** you are right; and I
don't think you are headed right./ **1191ff TMS** Well if you're ever going to think
(where you're going), do it now,/ after you got into trouble/ you'll remember what I
am tellin' you./ you'll say I was right *deleted*; **FC** For my words will come back too

OUS ESOPOOMENOI TROPHAS
KEDOMENOUS APH' HOON TE BLAST-
OOSIN APH' HOON T' ONASIN HEUR-
OOSI TAD' OUK EP' ISAS TELOUMEN
1200   ALL' OU TAN DIOS ASTRAPAN
KAI TAN OURANIAN THEMIN
DARON OUK APONETOI
OO CHTHONIA BROTOISI PHA-
MA KATA MOI BOASON OIK-
1205   TRAN OPA TOIS ENERTH' ATREI-
DAIS ACHOREUTA PHEROUS' ONEIDE

Shall not justice be done
by Zeus among men,
Shall a sound be borne under earth
1210   to the sons of Atreus?
          All
          is not well in his hall.
          His line dies out.

                        Antistrophe

HOTI SPHIN EDE TA MEN EK DOMOON NOSEI
1215   [DE] TA DE PROS TEKNOON DIPLE
PHULOPIS OUKET' EXISOU-
TAI PHILOTASIOOI DIAI-
TAI PRODOTOS DE MONA SALEUEI
ELEKTRA TON AEI PATROS
1220   DEILAIA STENACHOUS' HOPOOS
HA PANDURTOS AEDOON
OUTE TI TOU THANEIN PROME-
THES TO TE ME BLEPEIN HETOI-
MA DIDUMAN HELOUS' ERI-
1225   NUN TIS AN EUPATRIS HOODE BLASTOI

from above   be wise birds of omen
Tossed and alone

---

late,/ *deleted* .... late .... ; [You'll think of what I'm saying. Too]/ **1212 TMS**
their *deleted*/ **1226 TMS** the air *deleted*; **FC** very *deleted* wise birds of omen/ to be

                        Elektra
                         mourns
1230   constant aid hath she none
        As Philomel in grief
                        her sire's shade
                    so shamed of all the world
        nor cares to live or die,
1235   were he avenged.

        A child, indeed, of what race!   *Strophe* β
        Of what breed! heed, heed
        Nor would she live in shame

        (*Greek crescendo*)

1240   OUDEIS TOON AGATHOON YAR
        DZOON KAKOOS EUKELIAN AISCHUNAI THELEI
        NOONUMOS OO PAI PAI

        So fame's all-hovering   wing
        shall bear her praise
1245   for beauty of heart and mind
                        for constant faith

                    Nay, ere she die   *Antistrophe* β
                    may power come
        to lift her high,
1250   may yet her house be strong
        as Zeus gave law.

        DZOOIS MOI KATHUPERTHEN
        CHEIRI KAI PLOUTOOI TEOON ECHTHROON HOSON
        NUN HUPOCHEIP NAIEIS
1255   EPEI S' EPHEUREKA MOIRAI MEN OUK EN ESTHLAI
        BEBOOSAN HA DE MEGIST' EBLASTE NOMIMA
                TOONDE PHEROMENAN
        ARISTA TAI DZENOS EUSEBEIAI

---

observed *deleted*; [be wise]/ **1229 TMS** moans *deleted*/ **1236 FC** A child, indeed,
what race !; [of]/ **1237 FC** What breed!; [of]; [heed, heed]/ **1251 TMS** and Zeus

ORESTES

Eh, can any of you ladies
tell me: did we hear right and
1260   are we gettin' to where we wanted to come to?

*CHORUS (more or less automatically, mechanically
answering)*

Where do you want to get to?

(turning suddenly suspicous)

                AND WHY??
1265   What are you here for? .

ORESTES

Aegisthus. Where does he live,

(with morgue and double entente)

I been looking for him for SOME time.

CHORUS (gruffly)

1270   Well yuh can't blame the fellow that told you

(thumb over shoulder, pointing)

you got here.
This is it.

ORESTES

Well, eh . . . will any of you go in and . . . eh . . .
1275   say politely that we have respectfully got here.
                eh . . . on foot

---

give law/   **1258 FC** Eh, can any of you ladies tell me:/   **1259f TMS** if we're on the
right track and/ somewhere near to the end of it.?; (did we hear O.K. and come
where we wanted to get to)/   **1265 TMS** (What are you doin' here) *deleted*; what are
you poking into,/ AND WHY/   **1270 TMS** you *deleted*/   **1292 TMS** (If you want to)/

CHORUS

This unfortunate girl should
            She's of the family.

ORESTES *(dubiously)*

1280   Yes, lady? would you go say that some Phocaeans

(accent and tone, a bit grim and deliberate)

. . . have come for Aegisthus . . . . .

ELEKTRA *(half-sob)*

Oh God, I spose you've got the proof with you.

ORESTES

1285   Proof of what? Old Stroffy
         told us to bring the news of Orestes.

ELEKTRA *(sort of gasp)*

eeh, I was afraid so.

(in sort of glaze noticing her own hands)

1290   I'm all of a tremble.

ORESTES

We've got it here, all that is left of him
in this little jug, as you can see if you want to.

ELEKTRA

O. O it's all I can bear.

ORESTES

If it's Orestes you're crying for,
1295   If it's for his troubles,
         he's all there in the urn.

1296 FC (clutching at urn); (v. brief pause)/ 1299 FC (v. brief pause)/ 1302 FC

ELEKTRA

Oh give it me, for gods' sake, give it to ME

(hardly pause, but spoken staccato dividing the clauses)

It's the end of the line.
1300 we're all there together:
ashes.

(Elektra clutching at the urn which Pylades is carrying)

ORESTES

Give it to her, let her have it, whoever she is
She's not asking from spite,
1305 must be a friend or one of the family

ELEKTRA'S KEENING

All that is left me
my hope was Orestes
dust is returned me
1310 in my hands nothing, dust that is all of him,
flower that went forth

would I had died then
ere stealing thee from the slaughter
died both together
1315 lain with our father

Far from thy homeland
died far in exile
no hand was near thee
to soothe thy passing,
1320 corpse unanointed
fire consumed thee,
all now is nothing,
strangers have brought thee
small in this urn here

[which Pylades is carrying]/ **1303f FC** a gift/

1325   Sorrow upon me
      fruitless my caring

      I as mother and sister both
      thy nurse also ere thou hadst thy growth
      this was my past
1330   and swept away with thee
      ever to me
      thy summons came.

      all in a day
      and is no more.
1335   Dead Agamemnon, dead now my brother
      I am dead also, the great wind in passing
      bears us together.
      Mirth for our foemen.

      (anger now stronger than grief, for a moment: SPOKEN)

1340   And that bitch of a mother is laughing
      and they haven't sent back even the shape of him,
      but a ghost that cant do its job.

      Ajnn.   ajhn.

      (SINGS)

1345   thou the avenger, no more avenging
      born to misfortune, ashes avail not
      shadows avail not

      ahi,   ahi,
      bodiless
1350   brother that art not.

      (SPOKEN)

      The spirits love me no longer.
      you kept sending messages
      secretly, you would take vengeance.

1355   *(SINGS)*
      thy death, my dying

1359 TMS as ever over; **FC** *omitted/*

dred road thou goest
brother, my slayer
as ever above earth
1360   let death divide not

(singing to the urn)

Oimoi   Oimoi

take me in with you
I now am nothing, make place beside thee
1365   naught into naught, zero to zero
to enter beside thee
our fortune equal
death endeth pain.

CHORUS (sings)

1370   Mortal thy father, all men are mortal
Mortal Orestes,
All men must die.

ORESTES (speaks)

I can't stand much more of this

1375   *ELEKTRA (speaks)*

What's it to you

ORESTES

Good god, are you Elektra?

ELEKTRA

I am, and in misery.

ORESTES

Heaven help me.

1360 leave me not lost here; **FC** *omitted/* **1364 TMS** too *deleted/* **1368 TMS** dead
do not see, experience occasion of pain./ be afflicted./ **1381 FC** [very quick & angry]/

ELEKTRA

1380   What do you care about me?

ORESTES (very quick & angry)

what in hell have they done to you?

ELEKTRA

But are you sorry for ME

ORESTES

Unmarried, and such a life

ELEKTRA

1385   what are you lookin' at?
what you got to be sad about?
it isn't YOUR funeral

ORESTES

I didn't know the half of it

ELEKTRA

What's that got to do with ANYTHING?
1390   with anything we have said?

ORESTES

seeing you in this condition . . .

ELEKTRA

but you haven't seen anything yet
not the least part

1385 TMS what's the matter *deleted*/   **1387 TMS** (it isn't YOUR funeral); (you aint in mourning.)/   **1388 TMS** I didn't know half of it; **FC** [the]/   **1389 FC** *omitted*/ **1393 TMS** (seen few of my troubles); **FC** *omitted*/   **1397 TMS** How, what/ How do

ORESTES

Amn't I seeing enough, can there be anything more,
1395   more, worse?

ELEKTRA

Yes, living here with these assassins.

ORESTES

Whose assassins?

ELEKTRA

My father's, and me a slave.

ORESTES

Who compels you?

ELEKTRA

1400   They *say* she's my mother.

ORESTES

How? beats you, starves you?

ELEKTRA

Yes, and everything else.

ORESTES

And there's no one to help you, or stop her?

ELEKTRA

Nobody. Nothing but the dust that you've got there.

---

you mean it. What devilment *deleted/* **1398 TMS** EL/ patiently, and being explicit./
With my father's assassins. *deleted/* **1401 TMS** How? with violence and starvation.

ORESTES

1405   Poor dear, I've been sorry for you, a long time.

ELEKTRA

Well you're the first man that ever WAS.
and the only one.

ORESTES

Cause I've got the same trouble.

ELEKTRA

You mean you're a relative?

1410   *(after pause)*

where from?

ORESTES

Can you trust these people?

ELEKTRA

They're all right. You can trust 'em.

ORESTES

Give me back that jug, and I'll tell you.

ELEKTRA

1415   No, don't cheat me that way, for gods' sake.

ORESTES

Come on, you won't miss it.

---

deleted/ **1405 TMS** at the sight of you *deleted*; before *deleted*/ **1410f TMS** (where'd a relative come from?); **FC** *omitted*/ **1412 TMS** (are they well disposed?)/ **1417 FC**

ELEKTRA

Oh gosh, don't rob me, it's all I've got.

ORESTES

I wont. Give it here.

ELEKTRA

Oh poor Orestes, if I can't even bury you.

ORESTES

1420   Watch what you're saying.
you oughtn't to weep.

ELEKTRA

What when my brother's dead.

ORESTES

You oughtn't to talk that way about him.

ELEKTRA

What! Amn't I fit to

1425   *ORESTES (admiringly)*

You're fit for anything, but that isn't your job.

ELEKTRA

Not when I'm carrying his body here in my hands?

ORESTES

They're not his. That's a fairy tale.

Oh gosh, don't take it, it's all I've got,/ don't rob me/ **1419 TMS** (they wont even leave me your grave) *deleted*/ **1421 TMS** you got no right to be crying./ **1423 TMS**

ELEKTRA

Well where IS his grave.

ORESTES

1430   It aint. you dont bury people while they're alive.

ELEKTRA

What are you talking about?

ORESTES

Only the truth.

ELEKTRA

He's alive?

ORESTES

As I am.

ELEKTRA

1435   YOU?

ORESTES

Here's dad's ring.

ELEKTRA

O PHILTATON PHOS

ORESTES

what a day. I'll say it is.

ELEKTRA

And I hear you talking.

??? to him *deleted/* **1437 FC** Oo PHILTATOON PHOOS/ **1447 TMS** that *deleted/*

ORESTES

1440   Yes. we're agreed on that.

ELEKTRA

and I can hold onto you.

(embraces)

ORESTES

never let go.

ELEKTRA

Oh my dears, this is Orestes
1445   he wasn't really dead after all
he was just pretending, so he could get here.

CHORUS

Yes we can see him. makes one cry this does.

*ELEKTRA (singing starts sotto-voce, trembly; asides
spoken rhythmically with kettle drum accompaniment)*

heart, heart, heart thou art come

1450   *ORESTES*

yes, but keep quiet
for a bit just keep quiet

ELEKTRA

what for

ORESTES

somebody might hear there inside.

1448 TMS KETTLE-DRUMS; **FC** *deleted/*   **1450 FC** *omitted/*   **1452 TMS** PROSMENE

1455   *ELEKTRA (sings greek like Carmagnole. THIS song can*
       be burst into. Like wild Sioux injun war dance with
       tommy hawks)

       ALL' OU MA TEN
       ADMETON AIEN
       ARTEMIN

1460   Oh to hell with all the hens
       in the old hen house

       I aint afraid of hens
       cause they aint a bit of use.

       ORESTES

       bi god when the women get goin' it's Mars,

       ELEKTRA

1465   OTOTOTOTOI
       clear again, not to be ended,
       not to be forgotten,
       how our ill started, trouble began.

       ORESTES

       Don't I know it but
1470   to tell in its time
                   when the DEED recalls it

       ELEKTRA

       any time's right, now, I've hardly got my mouth free.

       ORESTES

       I'll say it is. And you damn well keep it free.

[all gk sung]; **FC** *omitted*/ **1464 TMS** speaks./ **1466ff TMS** our never ending
wrong, unclouded/ we cannot forget how it started/ **1471 TMS** deed/ **1472 FC**
[any time. & now @ last mebbe talk's free] *deleted*/ **1473 TMS** I agree. Now keep

ELEKTRA

How?

ORESTES

1475   By not talking too much at the wrong time.

ELEKTRA

You came when I'd given up hope
I got to keep quiet now?

ORESTES

I came as the gods moved me

ELEKTRA

That's the best the gods have done yet.

ORESTES

1480   Dont want to hold down on yr/ whoopee
But afraid you're overdoing it.

ELEKTRA

It's been so long, long, but the road's right,
you "deign" deign to show up here
now I can see you

---

it that way (free)/ **1476 TMS, FC** Who'd keep it in, if they weren't a dirty slouch/
Now you are here/ at last, must I still sit and grouch./ and mope/ **1478 TMS** I came
when I got the first hunch *deleted*; impelled *deleted*/ **1479 TMS** From the oracle?/
That's the best the gods have ever done yet *deleted*; If the gods put you up to it/ aint
that just wunnerful; Let ME witness the divine/ by my high-jinks/ **1480f TMS** I dont
want to stop down yr/ enjoyment/ an' I dont want you to give way to pleasure too
much; afraid you're too pleased; carousin'; your whoopee; Dont like to break up your
whoopee; dont go too happy YET; giving way too much to it/ euphoria; **FC** I dont
want to stop down your enjoyment/ But afraid you're overdoing it/ **1482ff TMS** Oh
a long long time to the right right road/ you "deign" (gosh) deign to show up here/ but
not me, seeing me full of toil./ considering all my worries. troubles; **FC** It's been so

1485   & you see my troubles
        but not me
                        DONT. . . . .

ORESTES

Dont what?

ELEKTRA

        Dont defraud me
1490   of the pleasure of seeing you here

ORESTES

damn well let anybody else try it

ELEKTRA

you dont mind?

ORESTES

Of course not, how cd/ I

ELEKTRA

        Oh dearest friends
1495   if now's to ear
        a voice I ne'er
        had hoped to hear

        If joy shall not
        burst forth at this

long, long,/ god bless the road,/ and then suddenly you come, and see all my troubles,/ Don't; find me LOOKING like this; [see what I've been thru]; [Its been so long,
long. but the road's right,/ now I can see you/ & you see my troubles]/ **1489f TMS**
dont defraud me, taking/ into neglecting, the pleasure of seein you/ You dont want
to stop my being glad you're back./ **1491 TMS** certainly not, and damn well let
anyone else try/ **1492 TMS** you like it?; You'll do what I tell you?/ **1493 TMS** how
cdn't I; (why wdn't I); sure I'll do what you tell me, why not/ **1500 TMS** and with-

1500   then ever dumb in wretchedness
            shd/ one live on in deep distress.

            Now thou art here
                        in full daylight
                        shall I not pour
1505   forth my delight,
            who ne'er in deepest woe
                        had forgot thee.

            *ORESTES (probably holding onto her, and trying to stop
            her gentle, but to get his hand on her jaw or mouth)*

1510   Yes, yes, but lay off the talk,
            You don't have to tell me how that bitch and Aegisthus
            are running all dad's place to ruin
            sluicin' it out in extravagance, luxury
            no time now for all that
1515   got to get on with the job
            tell me the best way to get to it,
            so I can fit the time,
            where to show, and where to hide
            to put an end to these bumptious bastids, and *how*.

1520   And dont look so damn happy
            that when we go in, she'll twig something is up

            Keep yr/ face mum, keep on weepin and bawlin'
            so she wont guess what we're up to,
            and laugh when we've finished the business
1525   and have got to some sort of freedom.

            ELEKTRA (breathlessly eager)

            Ye'ss, my dear, I just love it
            it's all yours and not mine

out sound; **FC** *deleted*/ **1506 TMS** never *deleted*/ **1513 TMS** in luxury and extrav-
agance/ in crazy expenses; runnin all dad's place to wrack *deleted*/ **1516ff TMS** to
hide and fool 'em/ talk will put out the nick of time/ show me where things are/
show we [*sic*] where things are at the moment; to hide and appear/ **1519 TMS**
(laughing enemies)/ **1522 TMS** when we go in/ **1527ff TMS** Yes *deleted*; What

I wont get in the way, I wont bother.
1530   You know Aegisthus is out, she's alone in the house now
don't worry about my lookin' happy
I loathe her,
                    And I've been weeping and crying
(for joy, but she needn't know that.)
1535   for the dead come alive
to do what I'd never have believed
so incredible that if father himself shd/ come
here alive I'd believe it
since you've got here this way
1540   tell me what you want done and I'll [follow
since] even alone I'd have done one or two things,
I'd have damn well thrown 'em out
or gone bust, been decently dead.

ORESTES (puts hand over her mouth)

1545   But HUSH
                    sounds as if someone
was coming out.

ELEKTRA

Yes, gentlemen, this is the way
nobody in this house will object to what you're bringing

1550   *TUTOR (furious)*

You BLOODY fools shut up
aint you got ANY sense whatever

you like, I like, and my pleasur's [*sic*] from you not me/ and I wdn' [*sic*] pain you the
least little bit/ for anything in the world/ (gt/ advantage)/ cause it wd/ run counter/
to the good luck now running./ our run of good luck./ (in good spirits)/ hex the good
spirits now being nice to us; **FC** *omitted*/ **1530 TMS** I spose you know Aesthius [*sic*]
is out/ no one but mother under that roof/ **1531 TMS** You needn't be afraid she'll
see me looking happy/ **1532 TMS** I've loathed her too much for too long/ **1533
TMS** for joy *deleted*; Besides I HAVE been cryin'/ **1534 FC** THAT/ **1536 FC** to do
what I never believe [?]/ **1537 TMS** as if father himself had come here alive/ **1542f
TMS** done it or perished *deleted*; finished the job or smashed./ **1549 TMS** throw

no more care for your lives
you aint on the brink of trouble,
1555   you are plumb bang in the middle
dont you know you're in danger
real danger, damn it.
If I hadn't been here keepin watch in this doorway
they'd already know what you're at before you get
1560   to it, before you get in there yourselves.
I've saved you that, anyhow,
and now if you've got thru with your gabble
& your blasted roaring
go in, But quiet,
1565   no good wasting time, either,
                   get it over.

ORESTES

What does it look like in there.

TUTOR

All jake, especially as nobody knows you

ORESTES

you've told 'em I'm dead?

TUTOR

1570   You're a ghost in hell as far as they go

---

you out; They wont throw out what you've got/ even if they "can't take it"; **FC** nobody
in this house will object to what you're bringing in/ **1553 TMS** do you want to get
killed *deleted*; Life may be cheap *deleted*/ **1554 TMS** you aint on the edge of danger/
1563f TMS get in; hurrahing; quit this hullabaloo, and go in; cut the cackle and quit
this blasted hullabaloo/ oh happy; quit yodling; **FC** exuberance *deleted*; [&]; but
quite; [B]/ **1565 TMS** no good wasting time; dont waste any time/ **1567 TMS**
How's it going in there; what are the chances in there. *deleted*/ **1568 TMS** O.K., and
the worse they do the better *deleted*; Good especially as nobody knows you *deleted*/
1569 TMS I suppose *deleted*/ **1570 TMS** They think you're in hell, and no bother;

ORESTES

And

      they're

            DEElighted.

What do they say about that?

TUTOR

1575   We'll go into THAT later.

and the worse they do, the better . . .

ELEKTRA

For gods' sake, who's this?

ORESTES

Can't you see

ELEKTRA

Haven't the foggiest . . .

ORESTES

1580   Well you handed me over to him.

ELEKTRA

What, what?

ORESTES

Well he sneaked me out of here

and got me to Phocis

ELEKTRA (gasps—tone of voice covers omitted words)

1585   The only one of the lot

who stood by me when father was murdered.

[You're a ghost in hell as far as they go]/ **1576 TMS** Eh *deleted*; **FC** the worse they

ORESTES

that's him. now hush.

ELEKTRA *(to Tutor)*

What a day
1590   YOU've done it alone.
You've saved the line. How did you get here
You've saved him and me
in all this misery, bless your hands

(grabs em, and presses them to her booZUM or cheeks)

1595   Oh gods bless the feet that brought you

(bit hysterical still)

how could you go on and not tell me,
and telling us all of those lies
and yet brought him.
1600   You seem more like a father,
OOH how I hated you.
                    What a dear.

TUTOR

Yes, yes, but now hush.
there's enough to fill nights and days
1605   we can go into that when the time comes

(then noticing Orestes and Pylades are still standing there)

What the hell are you doing here
Get on with it, she's alone
if you lose time, she'll have all the slaves up to fight you

do, the better/ **1588 TMS** (to PAID); **FC** *omitted*/ **1593 TMS** hand; **FC** [s]/ **1594 TMS** (I think she)/ **1595 TMS** your feet *deleted*/ **1600 TMS** You're *deleted*/ **1603 TMS** Now just a moment/ **1602 TMS** what; **FC** [W]/ **1604 FC** history *deleted*/ **1605 TMS** I'll tell you all of it later *deleted*/ **1606 TMS** gowking [*sic*] there; to Or and Pyl/ **1607ff** NOW we've got to get busy/ If you slow him up now, he'll/ you'll

1610   not only the servants but the palace guards
    the whole corps of them,
              and no pikers.

ORESTES (to Pylades who hasn't said a damn word.)

Come on, Pylades, cut the cackle.
1615   May the gods of the door be with us.

ELEKTRA (does the praying/ sings, sort of sing-song)

O King Apollo,
            HILEOOS
Favour us, favour us
1620   oft have I prayed thee
my little I gave thee
Phoibos, Lukeios
aid the right now
           let the gods show their godhead

CHORUS

1625   Mars breathing blood
           hounds that miss never their prey
miss never their spring, under the roof,
seeking the doers of ill, all ill, by stealth, by guile,
           Mars, breatheth blood,
1630   dogs that never miss their prey,
           the palace roof,
nor yet under-long to wait for the proof, of my presage.
           will, heart, and all.

have to fight all the guards *deleted*/ **1628 FC** seeking the doers of [ill,] all ill, by stealth, and *deleted* [by] guile,/ **1629 FC** see going forth the quarrelsome dred *deleted* Mars, breathing [eth] blood,/ **1630 FC** avenging *deleted*/ **1631 FC** ineluctable, enter *deleted*/ **1632 FC** not *deleted* [nor yet under-]/ **1638 TMS** ? or less/ **1639 FC**

*ELEKTRA (emerging from door, or slowly turning as part
of a pivoted door)*

1635   Oh my dears, my dears . . . . .
                    It's coming . . . . .
                          sh hh hhh

*(arm bent, hand level with shoulder, turns body sixty
degrees very slowly)*

SIGA PROSMENE

1640   *CHORUS (gt/ agitation)*

What? what?
                    whataretheydoing?

ELEKTRA

She's putting the wreath on the urn . . .
          and . . . and they're waiting.

CHORUS

1645   Whatchu come out for?

ELEKTRA

To keep watch for Aegisthus
          so he dont catch 'em.

KLYTEMNESTRA

AiHIII, nobody left,
          oohhhh assassins.

ELEKTRA

1650   Hear that?
                    Yes. dears, it's a noise.

omitted/ **1640 FC** *omitted/* **1650 TMS** (? gloat:)/ **1656 TMS** your husband/ Aga-

CHORUS

It's awful. Gimme the creeps.

KLYTEMNESTRA

aaaaah, Aegisthus. AE-gis-thus

ELEKTRA

Hear it, that's it again.

KLYTEMNESTRA

1655   Pity your mother

ORESTES (grim)

Did you pity father or me?

*CHORUS (now SINGS/ cry of misery/ keening on one note
or minimum rise and fall but monotonous and legato)*

1660   O city, o WRETCHED house
and the curse's tooth gnaws
        day after day

KLYTEMNESTRA

That's done it.

ELEKTRA

Hit her again.

KLYTEMNESTRA

1665   Twice, twice.
always twice.

memnon/ **1661f TMS** the curse is thinning out. OUT; and the curse/ day after day/
working out; and the curse gnaws, with the day; and the curse's tooth, gnaws by the

ELEKTRA (between her teeth)

Ajh. GOD, I wish it was Aegisthus.

CHORUS

In the end, weight unto weight
1670   fate works out to its end
They live who lie under ground
the blood of the dead, long dead
overfloods their slayers.
The dead hand drips Mars
1675   and the slain,
                    I can't blame 'em.

ELEKTRA

Orestes, how'd it go?

ORESTES

All right
The house is cleaned up
1680   if that oracle was on the square.

ELEKTRA

The bitch is dead?

ORESTES (sobered tone vs. Elektra's exultation)   ‹

You wont have any more trouble with mother.

day/ **1669ff TMS** Curses work out. Living lie low *deleted* They live, who lie under
ground/ The blood of the dead, long dead/ Overwhelms their slayers; Living the living, tho they lie low under ground. *deleted*; blood shed long ago,/ overfloods the slayers; They might be indeed, the hands/ drip Mars, and the victim/ blood, blood; **FC**
(singing); [Arah!] curses work[ed] out; They might be indeed *deleted* [and] the [dead
hand]; blood *deleted* and the victim *deleted* [slain] blood, blood. *deleted*/ **1677 TMS**
OO-restes, you've done it?; **FC** (how are you?) *deleted*; [how'd it go]/ **1678ff TMS**
As neat as Apollo said *deleted*; If Apollo said: neat/ the house is all tidy; **FC** if what
Apollo said is right *deleted*; [if that oracle was on the square; The house is clean[ed]
again *deleted* [up]/ **1682 TMS** (the excitement beginning to wear down. quietly.);

CHORUS

Sshh. Here comes Aegisthus.

ELEKTRA

1685   Back, can't you get back . . .

ORESTES

Where is the bloke?

ELEKTRA

Comin' up from the lower town, very chesty . . .

CHORUS

Quick, get into that vestibule, Hop!!
Good job so far. Now the next one.

ORESTES

1690   We'll do it. Don't worry.

ELEKTRA

Hurry, hurry.

ORESTES

Exit.

ELEKTRA

Now mine.

FC *omitted*; [sobered tone vs. E's exultation]/ **1684 TMS** (that's Aegistheus there in the open.); I see Aegistheus, there in the open./ **1685 TMS** Get back in *deleted*/

CHORUS

Now just a few polite words wd/ come in handy,
1695   so he wont guess he's rushin'
plumb bang into ruin,
                    an' he damn well deserves it.

AEGISTHUS (rather sissy voice, even a slight lisp)

Say you, where can I find these chappies from Phocis
1700   They say Orestes got killed in a chariot race
all messed up.

(to Elektra)

Here YOU, always so full of lip
it's mostly your business,
1705   you ought to know.

ELEKTRA

Sure I know. Think I dont care
about the last relative left me

AEGISTHUS

Well where are these chaps. Spit it out.

ELEKTRA

Inside, she's SO pleased to see 'em.

AEGISTHUS

1710   They said he was dead? How do they know.

ELEKTRA

They don't. They've only got the corpse with 'em.

1695 TMS see *deleted*; headin *deleted*/ **1718 TMS** if you think its enjoyable *deleted*/

AEGISTHUS

Can I get a look at it.

ELEKTRA (spoken slowly)

Yes.

1715   *(slight pause)*

It's an awful mess.

AEGISTHUS

Taint often you say anything to please me.

ELEKTRA

Go on and enjoy it, if that's the kind of thing you enjoy.

AEGISTHUS

Shut up.

1720   *(to Chorus)*

Get these doors open
so everybody in Mycene, and ARGOS
can see

(they open the big portone doors, slowly)

1725   if anybody had hopes of this man
they can now see him dead

(smacks his thigh)

and do what I tell 'em
and not wait till they're dead to find out.

1722 FC Argos/   **1724 FC** *omitted*/   **1725 TMS** was still hopin' *deleted*/   **1727 TMS** (does Aeg/ smack his thigh. probably); **FC** (smacks his thigh)/   **1729 TMS** and not wait to be licked. *deleted*; till I bump 'em off *deleted*; (not get ideas in their head)/

ELEKTRA

1730   Oh, I've learned that.
        No use goin' up against people in power.

AEGISTHUS

        O Zeus, that's a shape
        looks as if the gods didn't like him
        Here, I take that back. it aint lucky.
1735   Lift that napkin off his face, I'm one of the family
        in mourning.

ORESTES

        Lift it yourself. It's not my place
        to show these signs of love and devotion.

AEGISTHUS

        That's right.

1740   *(to Elektra)*

        go call Klytemnestra
        if she's at home.

ORESTES (as Aegisthus lifts napkin)

        She's right there. You needn'y look any further.

AEGISTHUS

1745   Gaaaaa!

ORESTES

        Whazza matter? haven't you seen her before?

1731 TMS no; **FC** [N]/ **1732 TMS** O Zeus, seen/ I see a sight/ not sent without
envy; **FC** I see a sight not sent without envy *deleted*; [that's a shape]/ **1735 TMS**
Take *deleted*/ **1740 FC** (to Electra)/ **1741 TMS, FC** Clytemnestra/

AEGISTHUS (in fury)

Who th' HELL. Damn, damn
I'm trapped.

ORESTES

1750   Haven't
                  you
                         ever learned
          That the
                  DEAD
1755   don't
                         DIE?

AEGISTHUS

Ajh. you're Orestes.

ORESTES

Ain't you clever. And it took you so LONG to find out.

AEGISTHUS

Here now, wait a minute, just let me

ELEKTRA

1760   DON'T
                  don't let him get a word in
          the brute's caught, what good's a half hour
          Kill him. Kill him.
                  and let the sextons cart him out
1765   get the stuff out of sight,
                  and let me forget it.

ORESTES (snarling)

GET ON IN THERE, stow the gab
you're in for it.

AEGISTHUS

1770   Why have I got to go in

(breaking)

and die in the dark
Why can't you do it here?

ORESTES

None of your business. You'll die
1775   where you killed my father.

AEGISTHUS

Fate. fate, under this damned roof of Pelops
everything happens here.

ORESTES

You'll get YOURS here at any rate.
I can tell you that much.

AEGISTHUS

1780   You didn't get that from your father.

ORESTES

Make a song about it?
            sing IN.

AEGISTHUS

I follow

*ORESTES (patient dragging voice, but sword point in
small of Aegisthus' back)*

1785   after you

AEGISTHUS

Hah. Fraid I'll give you the slip.

ORESTES

No, but you aren't dying for pleasure
you've got to go thru with it ALL.
It's a pity you can't all of you die like this
1790   and as quickly, everyone like you.
it wd/ save a lot of unpleasantness.

CHORUS (sings)

O SPERM' ATREOOS
                    Atreides, Atreides
1795   come thru the dark.

(speaks)

my god, it's come with a rush

(sings)

Delivered, Delivered.
1800   TEI NUN HORMEI TELEOOTHEN
        swift end
                    so soon.

1791 TMS fraid I'll give you slip/ **1792 TMS** ain't *deleted*; [aren't]/ **1800 TMS** TE
NUN ORME TELEOTHEN [(Loeb) 1.1510]/ **1802 FC** so soon. tenunteleothen.

NOTES

The numeration below corresponds to the line numbers of Pound's text. Line numbers for the Greek refer to the Loeb Classical Library edition *Sophocles*, vol. 2, trans. F. Storr (Cambridge, MA: Harvard University Press and London: William Heinemann Ltd., 1967). Further explanatory translations are taken from Richard C. Jebb., *Sophocles: The Plays and Fragments*, Part 6: *The Electra* (Cambridge: Cambridge University Press, 1907). Other abbreviations are for the following New Directions editions of Pound's works: *Confucius* (*C*), *Guide to Kulchur* (*GK*), *Literary Essays of Ezra Pound* (*LE*), *Selected Prose 1909-1965* (*SP*), *Ezra Pound: Translations* (*T*), and *Sophokles: Women of Trachis* (*WT*). Parenthetical references to *The Cantos of Ezra Pound* indicate canto and page numbers.

10f. *Mycene/ centre of the gold trade*: The insistent translation of the "Homeric" epithet for Mycenae, Μυκήνας τὰς πολυχρύσους, anticipates the emphasis that Pound will place upon economic considerations that he found crucial to the plot of Sophocles' drama. See notes to 11.74, 446, 533f.

26 *old Handy*: Pound derives the slangy nickname in a typical manner, by punning on the Greek ὦ φίλτατ᾽ ἀνδρῶν προσπόλων, "true friend and follower" (Jebb).

35 *to ask about doing right by father*: Pound's inquiries in the margins of **TMS** concerning the forms of the verbs μάθοιμ᾽ and ἀροίμην of 11.33-34 ("to learn/ maTH"; "aroimen/ 2nd. aor. mid. opt?") suggest that, at least when he began his translation, he did not have the commentary available in Jebb's bilingual edition, which elucidates the latter verb in detail.

39 *Kinky course, clean in the kill*: Pound's various attempts to render the Greek of 1.37 δόλοισι κλέψαι χειρὸς ἐνδίκους σφαγάς elicited Fleming's response in **FC**: "I think it is better here to let the word 'clean' take care of endikous." (Jebb translates "righteous.")

52 *with libations and all my pretty curls*: Pound's inquiry in **TMS** as to the tone of the Greek in this passage ("ironic?") initiated a dialogue that would preoccupy him and his collaborator throughout the translation. Fleming replied in **FC**: "This is a hard place like all the ritual passages; I don't think there is any irony in the Greek; here the tone of the translation clashes with the original; in the translation the statement of Orestes has got to be ironic and so, throughout, the clash will have to be *used*; the modern speech will struggle against the ritual and sometimes win and sometimes be overridden by the pressures of the dramatic situation itself towards ritualistic expression."

61 *I don't suppose the lie will ruin our luck*: Fleming notes in **FC**: "Orestes is afraid to play dead; I think a more direct expression of this fear would help."

74 *the old rule of abundance*: This very Poundian turn of phrase translates ἀρχέπλουτον (Jebb explains "*master* of my possessions" or "having *ancient* wealth") and is inspired by a concept central to the poet's economics. See "The ABC of Economics," *SP*, 234.

79f. *the time./ Best leader men have*: Fleming preferred Pound's first attempt upon the Greek at 11.75-76, and he remarked in **FC**: "Of the alternates I think this best/ Jebb has the right meaning: 'for so occasion bids, chief ruler of every enterprise for men'."

188ff. *ITUN . . . DAKRUEIS*: The progression of the Greek suggests a probable echo for Pound of Aeschylus, *Agamemnon*, 1144, and recalls significant moments in his own *Cantos*. See 4/13-14 and 76/460.

230 *every message I get is a cheat*: Pound was apparently baffled by lexical and grammatical difficulties in 11.169-70 of the Greek. He referred in **TMS** to a "crib" that could possibly be distinct from the Loeb or Jebb: "crib/ FROM/ from me/ erXomai/ Eldt/ to me." He could have been misled by the vagueness of the Loeb ("All those messages are vain—"), but Ellendt's lexicon and Jebb's version seem to be explicit at this point.

TMS suggests that the poet was no less exercised by the attendant thought of Henry Luce's publishing empire.

233ff. *THARSEI MOI* etc.: Pound's stage direction for this "STROPHE" (in fact, an antistrophe in the Greek) elicited Fleming's somewhat incredulous response in **FC**: "(all Greek no English?)."

274 *horrible*: In **TMS** Pound worried the full burden of the Greek phrase at 1.204, ἔκπαγλ᾽ ἄχθη: "(eKpagl) ex/ pan/ l? aXthos/ load voc/?; ?table atmosphere while getting Ag/ drunk enough to kill??"

294 *Is there any limit to the nature of misery*: In addition to the variant versions of 1.235 in the Greek (καὶ τί μέτρον κακότατος ἔφυ . . .), **TMS** includes these marginalia: "kakoTATOS (e.e.c. construction. HYPEREKTESO, 217." Apparently, Pound initially construed the genetive noun κακότατος as a superlative adjective, but then mistook it as an idio-syncratic compound on the model of Sophocles' ὑπερεκτήσω in 1.217. He seems then to have made the analogy to coinages to be found in the poetry of Cummings.

297 *respect*: In puzzling out the Greek word ἔντιμος of 1.239, Pound added in **TMS**, "os as alogos," thus reminding himself and Fleming that the apparently masculine ending of a compound adjective qualifies fem-inine nouns as well.

300 *keening*: **TMS** records Pound's very literal imaginings of the Greek phrase at 11.242-43, πτέρυγας/ὀξυτόνων γόων, "the wings of shrill lamentation" (Jebb): "goon/ Ag's death, Clty's character. wing each. 243."

309ff. TMS suggests that Pound struggled with this speech through-out: "HAS R.F. ANY suggestions??" The translator was confused by the contraction ἄγω of 1.259 ("H'ago:: with this rottenness agos? Loeb mis-prints? or variants? agos, HAGoo"), but he appeared to be more certain of the tone in the noun εὐφρόνην on the same line: "irony in euphronEn."

320ff. The Greek apparently posed special difficulties at 11.264-65 ("rule or attain/ arXO lambano/ be governed, attain") and exacted from Pound several variant attempts at translation.

330f. *a whore, a mother? call it/ a concubine*: **FC** records Fleming's scrupling at Pound's interpretation of the Greek in 11.273-74: "The three words whore, mother, concubine taken together define the matter pretty well, but how do they go together?"

333 *the curse*: **TMS** notes Pound's recourse to his lexicon for the word ἐρινὺν at 1.276: "(Elendt/ vengeance) prefer curse/ cf/ 1.500/513." The latter reference is to the choral ode for which Pound was to translate the word as "Vengeance." See 1.549 in the text.

337f. Between these two lines, **TMS** registers this interruption in the translation, "(13th Gamelion, Jan)/ conjectured," and the following handwritten lines: "the salt/ full force/ of/ Cronus/ Time moves [on, an?]/ [ponce?]/ [an?] easy god./ Orestes not/ Nor Death—who is lord over/ αχερων/ Time is an easy god/ Orestes [is?] not/ nor the lord of αχεRον/ nor is Death/ who is lord/ of AχERων"

356 *of all the dastardly yellow pests*: In reference to the Greek phrase ἡ πᾶσα βλάβη at 1.301, lexical marginalia in **TMS** further suggest: "blab/ harm damage, 'total loss'."

373 *he wont let you down*: **TMS** attests to Pound's dissatisfaction with "friends" as a translation of φίλοις at 1.322: "philois, stronger here."

376 *DOWN THERE*: In addition to the stage direction, Pound suggested in **TMS** that there should be an "echo" of the Greek in 1.327, τοῖς κάτω νομίζεται.

401 *Need we add cowardize to all the rest of this filth*: To the lines "SPLENDOUR/ IT ALL COHERES" in his later translation of Sophocles' *Trachiniae*, Pound appended the following in a footnote: "This is the key phrase, for which the play exists, as in the *Elektra*: 'Need we add cowardice to all the rest of these ills?' or the "T' as inventé la justice" in Cocteau's *Antigone*. And, later: "Tutto quello che è accaduto, doveva accadare" (*WT*, 50n.). The last reference is to a memoir of 1943 attributed to Mussolini, translated as *Notebook of Thoughts in Ponza and La Maddalena* in the Australian magazine *Edge*, 4 (March 1957), 10-26. All four texts are alluded to in the *Cantos*, e.g., at 85/559, 86/564 and 87/571-72. See also "Jean Cocteau Sociologist," *SP*, 435-36. The phrase from *Elektra* also came to serve as an epigraph for the Poundian leaflet *Four Pages*, published in Galveston, Texas.

406f. *That honours the dead, if the dead get any joy out of that*: **TMS** reveals that Pound consulted Goodwin's *A Greek Grammar*, as well as Ellendt's lexicon, in his attempt to translate 11.355-56 in the Greek: "Elendt/ attribute honour to the dead . . esti (existence or possibility. Good/ 144.5)"

429 *for the god's sake*: Pound's translation of the idiom πρὸς θεῶν at 1.369 elicited Fleming's demurral in **FC**: "(why not just 'for god's sake?' The 'gods' in this play are going to have to fall in with the other chips, aren't they? as in The *Second Shepherd's Play*)." Pound retorted in a marginal note: "no not a monotheistic cosmos. sounds same but may as well be printed in key."

446 *What for*: Pound's undertranslation of the Greek ὅπως πάθῃς τί χρῆμα at 1.390 hardly conveys the gloss on the noun that he recorded in his copy of the Loeb edition: "χρ thing, act, wealth." He had also underscored the verb χρῶ at 1.44, and both gestures reflect his years-long preoccupation with derivatives of the verbs χράω and χράομαι. See especially his commentary on Aristotle's *Nicomachean Ethics* in GK, 304-41, 357, 359, and in the *Cantos* at 87/570, 104/739, 106/753.

456ff. *fail . . . fail*: **TMS** notes Pound's concern in regard to the verbs πεσεῖν and πεσούμεθ' at 11.398-99 (both translated "fall" by Jebb and the Loeb). Fleming wrote in **FC**: "I like 'fail' for pesein in both places; the change would not be heard anyhow." To which Pound added, "yes."

460 *I am sure*: Pound's variant renderings of the Greek at 1.400 are explained by his marginal inquiry in **TMS**: "OIDA? very strong?"

470 *all roasted*: **FC** records Fleming's appreciation of Pound's turn on the word for "burnt offerings": " 'roasted' seems good for empura."

471 *Mother told me to go water the grave*: The studied naiveté of
Pound's version of the Greek at 1.406 (compare "Here comes a man with
a wreath on" in *WT*, 10, or even the *Cantos*' "sickly death's-heads at 1/
3) elicited this memorandum from Fleming in **FC**: "Here is another ritual puzzle; 'water' brings in All Saints or Decoration Day; my own feel-
ing is that the anacronisms [*sic*] are all to the good *if* they can bring
about an interesting juxtaposition (As you know, the theatre is, for me,
a place where all kinds of 'meetings' can occur: the drama itself being
the occasion and the shape of the meeting—if that says what I mean.)"
Pound responded, "OK."

481 *down or up*: Pound copy of the Loeb contains an earlier attempt
at 1.416 in the Greek: "down 'em or up 'em." The heavy markings in his
text here and on subsequent pages reveal the poet's earnest struggles
with the most elemental of lexical and syntactical matters in his efforts
to grasp Sophocles' language.

496 *plant gifts or carry lustrations*: In **TMS** Pound mused upon
11.433-34 in the Greek: "KTERISMA, Eldt/ fun/ gifts OR rites. HISTEMI
cause to stand cf/ Nishikigi loutron/ washing bath expiatory." Apart
from lexical matters, these notes recall Pound's translation of the Japanese noh play "Nishikigi," published in 1916, which concerns the ghost
of a disappointed lover whose funeral cave is thronged with "nishikigi"—"wands used as a love-charm" (*T*, 286). Pound evidently likened
these to the Greek κτερίσματα, gifts dedicated to the dead.

514 *the tip of one of yr/ curls*: The margins of **TMS** suggest that
Pound had difficulties with this entire speech but succeeded in distin-
guishing the Greek contraction κἀπὶ at 1.445 as "kai epi." He remained
perplexed by the "effect" of κρατὸς at 1.449. Fleming responded in **FC**:
"(kratos is gen. of kras meaning head, summit) tip."

519 *But kneel and beg*: Pound was evidently confused by the verb
αἰτοῦ at 1.453. **TMS** has "??Aitou pardoning our faults." Fleming explained in **FC**: "aitou is beg."

533f. *if the old screw gets wind of it/ she'll make me pay for the risk*:
As the variants of these lines indicate, the Greek at 11.470f. touched off
very sensitive associations for Pound. In **TMS** he seemed convinced that
ἡ τεκοῦσα implied not "mother" but "usuress," and that the entire Greek
phrase might allude to nefarious lending or insurance practices in ancient Greece: "HE not my or our tekousa/ not teknousa tokkos/ interest/
?sea insurance. idiom??" The word was for Pound derived from τόκος,
not τίκτω. In **FC** Fleming ventured: "I don't think the idea of usury is in
the Greek, but the epithet fits the notion that the house of Ateus has
fallen on vulgar days."
Pound retorted: "τοκκος. τεκοῦσα I am very firm on this shade of

meaning haemerodeis nidzein etc. dunno if Salmasius can be found in this country." For some of Pound's representative remarks on Claudius Salmasius, or Claude de Saumaise (1588-1653) and his *De Modo Usurarum*, see *SP*, 272-73, 323.

535ff. The many variants for this chorus suggest Pound's dissatisfaction with his translation. He wrote in **FC**: "chorus not in final form = revise when we get to music."

592 *keeps you from making dirt on your friends' doorstep*: **TMS** records Pound's attempt to visualize Elektra's precise position: "epeXo Eld. crib θυριαν out of doors." Fleming in **FC** suggested: "? more freely the family doorstep" for the Greek of 1.518.

594f. *a lot of brash talk/ to a lot of people*: In his attempt to render the force of the Greek πολλὰ πρὸς πολλούς at 1.520, Pound asked in **TMS**: "where does Storr get polla: many times." The Loeb version reads, "many a time/ To many . . . ."

598 *you and your gang*: Pound was apparently perplexed by the Greek structure καὶ σὲ καὶ τὰ σά at 1.522. He wondered in **TMS**: "ta sa your people?? yr possessions. (Kl/ minimizing? or what??)"

605f. *I killed him/ yes, me, and a good job*: An Aeschylean echo impinges here upon Pound's translation of the Greek at 11.526-27. Compare his early version of *Agamemnon*, 1404-06: "This is Agamemnon,/ My husband,/ Dead by this hand,/ And a good job. These, gentlemen, are the facts" (*LE*, 270). See also the *Cantos*, 58/323; 82/523.

629 *even if we split on it*: The variant line indicates Pound's uncertainty as to the tone to be taken in Klytemnestra's opening speech. In **TMS** he wondered: "KL/'s tone?? prissy in speech tough in act?? How vulgar? ought she be? after all Tindarida. sister or 1/2"

Fleming replied in **FC**: "You have here the question: how vulgar ought she to be? The vulgarity, lack of emotional control are the mess Electra and her brother have to clean up; so I don't suppose she can be too vulgar as long as the vulgarity remains dramatic."

655 *not according to hunting rites*: Pound apparently misconstrued the Greek at 11.568-69. Jebb gives: "he shot it, and chanced to utter a certain boast *concerning its slaughter*" (emphasis mine). He noted in **TMS**: "kata sfagas/ chance of the striking/ ekkompasas/ boast." The Greek phrase "κατὰ σφαγάς" was to reemerge in the "Rock Drill" section of the *Cantos*, apposite a reference to Giuseppe Mazzini's primer of ethics "On the Duties of Man" (89/603). See also "Agamemnon killed that stag, against hunting rites" (89/602).

696 *from your side at least*: The earlier variant elicited some hesitancy from Fleming in **FC**: "Should be pitched higher?" Pound agreed that it "shd" and revised the line in order to make it "tougher."

707 *dirty workers teach dirty work*: **FC** records Fleming's opinion that Elektra's is "an important speech."

709 *and NOT done*: Pound's otherwise incomprehensible turn upon the Greek of 11.622-23 may have been influenced by his own line composed at Pisa: "Here error is all in the not done" (81/522).

713 *nomina sunt consequetia rerum*: In **TMS** Pound instructed: "BROKEN letter in text." Professor Noel Stock informs me that in his correspondence Pound seemed to associate this Latin tag ("words are the consequence of things") with the writings of Richard of St. Victor (d. 1173). It is also reminiscent of Pound's nearly contemporaneous translation from the Confucian "Analects": "the proper man's words must cohere to things, correspond to them (exactly)" (*C*, 249).

714 *By the Virgin*: Pound's copy of the Loeb records his gloss upon the Greek δέσποιναν Ἄρτεμιν at 1.626: "Jugoslav Gospodin." He later employed this title of respect in reference to Sophocles' Deianeira when he quoted from the *Trachiniae* in "Rock Drill": "gospoda Δηάνειρα" (87/571).

716 *tells me*: The variant "tell(s)" reflects Pound's question in **TMS**: "? can it be twisted to chorus or has she got to address Clyt??"

758 *Gruss Gott*: This salutation echoes an autobiographical account included in the "Pisan Cantos" of Pound's visit to his daughter in the Italian Tirol in 1943. See 78/478. Fleming remarked in **FC**: "The PAID/ ["Tutor"] appears here as a comic character—good!"

763f. **FC** erroneously attributes these lines to "EL/" ("Elektra").

766 *Oooh, that's the end*: In **FC** Fleming noted after this line: "The mingling here of tragedy, comedy, and burlesque will take lots of rhythm to hold it in—building up beyond the horse race speech to the chorus where EL/ shows her misery (From now on the whole movement accelerates)."

861ff. *Ooooh, he's dead* etc.: Among other difficulties with the Greek of 11.788-90, Pound singled out his puzzlement at the words τὴν σὴν ξυμφοράν, "thy fortune" (Jebb): "sEn can apply to Kl/ as well as to Or??"

884 *00 TALAIN' EGOO*: In **TMS** Pound indicated that the Greek at 1.807 should "echo" here, and he wondered further, "aria/gk?" Fleming responded in **FC**: "I think the Greek begins here to move up to the choral part which is *very* excited—EL/ and the XO/ pulling *against* each other— to use the Greek and English contrapuntally here would surely be all right."

The translation of this speech greatly condenses the original Greek.

903 *don't tell me about life after death*: In **TMS** Pound mused upon the adverb φανερῶς, "manifestly," at 1.833 ("? phanerOs, sure/ apparitions, not "manifestly dead"/ hope for apparitions of those in hell"), but his translation seems to have given way to a "Confucian" influence. See the *Cantos*' "Kung" who "said nothing of the 'life after death'" (13:59) and Pound's version of the "Analects" at *C*, 239.

947f. *but to die so* etc.: **TMS** records Pound's observations upon the Greek at 11.861ff.: "(all these circumflexes.) quiquonque [*sic*] meurt meurt à douleur [whoever dies, dies in grief]/ why the hell slow claw equals swift foot??" Pound's question alludes to the epithet χαλάργοις and to the fact that the noun χηλή may mean a crab's "claw" as well as a horse's "hoof."

950 *whose death was unforeseen*: Regarding the Greek adjective ἄσκο-πος at 1.864, Pound reasoned in **TMS**: "askop/ unseen, insolito/ the like as was never seen."

954 *AHI*: Pound added in **TMS**: "as we dont circumflex in english/ only way to do as Debusy in Chas/ dOrleans setting/ chorus soft counter point. ahi, ahi voices as instruments during most of this."

974 *has anyone LIVING*: In **TMS** Pound explained in regard to 1.883 in the Greek: "i.e. EL/ thinks Cr/ has seen O's ghost/ position of the brotOn." Fleming suggested the translation "ghost" in **FC**, to which Pound answered: "as distinct from."

990 s.d.: Pound's reference here to the Japanese "Noh" anticipates his even more explicit use of the Japanese dramatic conventions in his translation of Sophocles' *Trachiniae*.

994 *who on earth cd/*: In **TMS** Pound specified this "repeat" and added: "gk/ word order more important than syntactic coherence"—a remark somewhat reminiscent of the prescription penned thirty years previously, in regard to Aeschylus: "certainly more sense and less syntax (good or bad) in translating Aeschylus might be a relief" (*LE*, 273).

1047 *finish it up*: Pound rejected the reading ποεῖν, "act" (Jebb), at 1.947. **TMS** notes: "stronger than poein (take variant from Ellendt. TE-LEIN)."

1053f. *hoping he'd come and . . . wipe out the murder*: Pound was evidently intrigued by the noun and verb at 1.953 πράκτορ' ἵξεσθαι (which he obviously mistook as a form of the verb ἵζω): "?HiZo praktOr not hiemi??/ ?? idiom/ sit, as in judgement?? technical term." **TMS** also notes his opinion: "Hardest speech in the play to manage." Pound even wondered at 11.965-66 in the Greek: "will closer trans/ improve??"

1102 *the free born*: Pound worried about the "stage appeal" of translating τοῖς καλῶς πεφυκόσιν at 1.989. In **TMS** he explained: "really means: NOBLESSE OBLIGE but I dont see how one can use it."

1120 *to break a man*: Confronted with the word ἑλεῖν at 1.1001, Pound noted in **TMS**: "(HELEIN not in lexicon) ? destroy." Pound did not recognize this form of the verb αἱρέω, yet he evidently recalled the punning epithets for Helen of Troy in *Agamemnon*, 689-90, ἑλέναυς ἕλανδρος ἑλέπτολις. See also the *Cantos*, 2/6; 7/24-25.

1128f. *dead/ Death's*: Between these lines in **TMS**, Pound wrote: "STRONGLY object to Wangerism [*sic*] i.e. making so much and so many kinds of noise audience gets excited and dont know what's going on hence opposed to SINGING save in emotional passages where nature of emotion is comprehensible, i.e. quite simple, usually elegiac (not always, as in THARSAI MOI, etc. but simple and not doing with intellectual complex.)"

1134f. *I'll keep my mouth shut . . . I think it's, all of it, useless*: In **TMS** Pound glossed these lines: "Stendhal/ or dans ce genre on n'emeut que par la clarté." See *LE*, 54.

1141ff. *Just as I thought* etc.: In **TMS** Pound recorded: "next clause literal/ adds nothing?" And he once again emphasized that "order of thought in gk more important than syntax." See note 994.

1144ff. Both **TMS** and **FC** ascribe this speech to "XO/" (the Chorus) and not, as the Greek texts indicate, to Chrysothemis.

1174 *I'd rather die*: In regard to the verb ζῆν at 1.1043, Pound remarked of his translation in **TMS**: "?? overemphasis on zEn/ I dont think so. ?? but mebbe."

1180 *You just dont understand what I'm saying*: Numerous question marks in **TMS** suggest Pound's dissatisfaction with this rendering of the Greek at 1.1048. He explained to Fleming that it was a "paraphrase." Fleming reassured him in **FC**: "phronein can mean 'understand' and then this trans. is strictly literal."

1192ff. *If you ever aim* etc.: Pound was equally displeased with his initial attempts at this speech. He noted in **TMS**: "very weak end and take off for chorus. got to be improved. corresponds to end of an act."

1195ff. *TI TOUS* etc.: In **TMS** Pound instructed that the "1st / Strophe in gk/ all of it" should be sung along with a "brief summary sung in eng/." He added: "any how, scaffold or draft."

1251 *as Zeus gave law*: Pound was apparently confused by the "syntax" in the antistrophe of 11.1090ff., yet he glossed the sense in **TMS**: "we havent found you in luck but observing highest piety to Zeus."

1257 *EUSEBEIAI*: Regarding the pronunciation of the last word in the chorus (εὐσεβείᾳ at 1.1097), Pound directed in **TMS**: "short chop chop on the final a."

1285 *Proof of what*: Pound explained in **TMS**: "slight paraphrase here."

1293 *all I can bear*: In **TMS** Pound noted of the word ἄχθος at

1.1116, "ambiguity in the aXthos two meanings"—presumably both the "burden" Orestes is bearing and Elektra's "woe."

1302 s.d.: In **TMS** Pound recorded some discomfort with Orestes' words at 1.1123 in the Greek: "prosPHerontes/ offer, ?to keep/ cant visualize the 'bring it forward' idea in crib and Loeb. much better stage to have her clutch at it in first place."

1306 *ELEKTRA'S KEEENING*: In **TMS** Pound provided these preliminary suggestions for eventual performance: "(I think sung from the start) possibly in antiphony, El/ solo in english and line by line, greek echo from chorus. El/ gradual crescendo/ chorus starting pianissimo/ contrapunto. (Chorus probably, yes, I think per force solo at start, and more voices later.) Vocal orchestration. for the emotional passages translate the total emotion of the whole speech. for mental conflicts: the meaning, exact meaning word by word. or dans ce genre on n'emeut que par la clarté [See note 1134f.] (possible ameliorations WHEN the music is actually written)"

1312ff. *would I had died* etc.: Pound reiterated in **TMS**: "(lines interspersed with the gk/ of chorus in contrapunto.) probably, ut supra line against line. not paragraph vs/ pp/ note all the sense in general/ not the close lock of the dialogs."

1326 *fruitless my caring*: Pound remarked in **TMS**: "(language of feelings, not lang/ of action)"

1327ff. *I as mother* etc.: In **TMS** Pound marked this stanza "(provisional)."

1358ff. *brother, my slayer . . . but death divide not*: **TMS** suggests that Pound sensed an "antithesis" at 11.1157-58 in the Greek: "PHileIto philTates. what's in BIG Liddel." [LSJ: ἐξαφαιρέω : ἐξαφείλετο].

1390ff. **TMS** reveals Pound's attempts to "PARSE" the exchange between Elektra and Orestes at 11.1187-89 in the Greek: "diagignosco found it out from something we've said/ what looking at mourn not the past but now/ not my past but present in the what of what we hv/ sd/"

1396f. *living here with these assassins/ Whose assassins*: In **TMS** Pound again registered his difficulties with the Greek, here at 11.1190-91: "TEXT???? or meaning of suntroFos. (eZesEmEnas/ from?? anyhow, clause cant add anything, and only clogs."

1417 *don't rob me*: Pound asked in **TMS**: "?? form of ZELE not in vocab/?" His inquiry refers to [ἐ] ξέλῃ at 1.1208.

1448 s.d.: **TMS** included the direction "KETTLE-DRUMS," which was deleted in **FC**.

1455 s.d.: In **TMS** Pound added: "probably keep the drums till the end/ mebbe with intervals. and beat the gk/ scansion probably if it fits/ NO other MOVEMENT possible/"

1458 *ADMETON*: Pound complained in **TMS**: "an by cripes they try to tone down the AdmEton/ to VIRGIN// holy makeli. . . . ." See the Greek, l. 1239.

1469 *Don't I know it*: The ordering of lines in **FC** is very confused because Fleming noted a "speech transposed here." Pound then compounded his slight mistake by attempting a major restructuring of 11.1456-70. I have retained the order of the Greek as it was more nearly followed in **TMS**. There Pound wrote, in any event: "(provisional as scaffold) WHOLE of the greek 1232. probably to 1287 sung/ sometimes?? by El or Or/ sometimes by XO/ doubling El or Or/ who sometimes sing. sometimes put in explanatory pithy asides."

1472 *any time's right*: Evidently dissatisfied with this entire passage, Pound wrote in **TMS**: "FIVE lines/ here, want Jebb/ and all possibilities of MEANING before I bother further. also next speech, and ennepein dika (technical law jargon) free mouth." In **FC** Fleming supplied Jebb's translation of 11.1246-56 in the Greek, from which Pound derived his own 1.1472.

1476f. *You came . . ./ I got to keep quiet*: Pound remarked upon this line and its variant in **TMS**: "(its the reply, possibly inversion of the To hell with all the hens. (Question of TIME duration. If cho/ doubles by singing BOTH gk/ and eng/ this cd/ be spoken. The EMOTION in this antistrophe is ANTI that of the strophe/ not necessary to give both in same register of trans/ rhythmic speech with kettle-drums, possible. got to have MEANING clear, before deciding. of ALL words/ gamut of emotion very great from 1232////"

1478 *I came as the gods moved me*: Having just made an earnest schoolboy's inquiry into 1.1260 in the Greek ("crib and glos/ take aZian as adj/ form . . . construction is??? acc/ fem/"), Pound proffered this philological judgment upon the text at 1.1264: "HOTE/ as mss/ cert better than Jebb's eute/"

1483 *"deign" deign*: As the variant "(gosh)" suggests, Pound confirmed in **FC** that his translation in quotation marks was "kidding the crib" at 11.1273ff. (Jebb: "O thou who, after many a year, hast deigned thus . . ."). Pound also remarked the words ἰδὼν φανῆναι : "visible = suggestion to eye? find me LOOKING like this/ shame for her rags."

1489f. *Dont defraud me/ of the pleasure*: Noting the Greek words ἡδονῇ at 1.1272 and ἁδονάν at l. 1277, Pound asked in **TMS**: "Why the hell at ETA 1272 and an alpha here. Or/ got to talkin with a furrin accent or wottellll????"

1494ff. *Oh dearest friends/ . . . had forgot thee*: In **TMS** Pound appended to these lines: "Yrs/ v.t. Thos/ Moore," presumably acknowledging a parody of the Irish poet, translator and lyricist (1779-1852).

1540f *[follow/ since]*: **FC** suggests that Pound did not approve of the "language" here.

1549 *nobody in this house will object*: Not recognizing the verb ἤδο-μαι at 1.1325, Pound speculated in **TMS** upon ἡσθείη : "HEStheiE, not in vocab/ Loeb: bitter Hestia/hearth or receive *Hesthie* Histemi be in condition to receive/ stand receiving."

1615 *May the gods of the door be with us*: In **TMS** Pound wrote: "cant make sign of the cross, but possibly somebody knows the correct gesture/ must ask." **FC** added, apparently after Fleming had spoken with Pound: "Ask Bowra or George Tyler."

1617ff. *O King Apollo* etc.: Pound noted in **TMS**: "not sung in the orig/ str/ begins with XO/ (this is in the gk/ like the drone of a prayer, still in ritual, just as gabbled as still in Kat/ churches."

1625 *Mars breathing blood*: In **TMS** Pound remarked of this chorus: "DAMN/ rhythm a twister."

1639 *SIGA PROSMENE*: Pound here registered a deliberate echo of *Agamemnon*, 1344 and of his own *Cantos* (5/19) by transliterating the Greek phrase in l. 1398.

1657 *Did you pity father or me*: Both **TMS** and **FC** attribute to Orestes the words spoken by Elektra at 11.1411-12 in the Greek.

1661 *and the curse's tooth gnaws*: **TMS** reveals that Pound was, understandably confused by the Greek at 11.1413-14: "(crib and Loeb diametric opposite meanings. OUT, eroding/ ELLENDT reads PHTHinein. phTHinein."

1665 *Twice, twice*: The Greek of 1.1416, ὤμοι μάλ᾽ αὖθις elicited these responses from Pound: in the margin of his Loeb, "echo Aeschylus"; in **TMS**, "echo of Aeschylus when Ag/ is killed"; in **FC**, "note echo of Aeschylus/ got to explain in *Preface*." See, too, the echo of *Agamemnon*, 1345 in the *Cantos* (5/19).

1669ff. *In the end* etc.: For the chorus of 11.1419ff., Pound remarked in **TMS**: "general statements from Xo. HyperZaireo// divulge. what in big/ dic. pareisin/ the presence of the ghost of Ag/? Can we make 'em see the DEAD WITH Orestes?" He noted, too, of the Loeb version: "neither THE curses, nor live AGAIN in text."

To his revised translation in **TMS** Pound appended the following general notes:

"Perfectly easy to throw (magic-lantern) ghost of Agamemnon on white surface (flat white marble beside door or opening behind Orestes. ITS hands dripping RED blood. probably better on wall by door so as to be visible to all seats in audience.

"re/lines 1281 seq./ and for Polly [Mrs. Fleming] also/ control the language/ not hv/ lang control you. Get the MEANING, then there are dozens of ways to express it. dont let rhythm control you. control IT.// O.K. to Klut's first entrance. 1426 EI eTHespisen/// beginning of O's doubt of the oracle foreboding later madness.

"LEX/ 1. there must be real person speaking possible speech NOT goddam book-talk. 2. Must be the stage SEEN, the position of the person speaking and their movements. 3. Modification of speech MINIMUM or NONE for the sung parts. They shd/ be as straight as Drink to me only-with thine eyes. BUT cantabile. 4. When danced, the foot-beat must be indicated BY the words, from them to the tune. 5. for the sung part the translation need NOT adhere to literal sense (intellectual) of the original but must be singable IN THE EMOTION of the original.

"Note for finale/ The big double doors are open so the WHOLE auditorium can see Klut's bier, and the scene of lifting the cloth/ Aeg/ is driven thru another door into the inner room where Ag/ was murdered./ Restraint of S/ in NOT including Aeg's death in actual play. One murder enough in action. One implied, with no doubt about it, but not visibly demonstrated. one doesn't at first realize that it is not actually in the text.

"poetry = see/ stage/ = & hear"

1680 *if that oracle was on the square*: In **FC** Pound again addressed the importance for him of 1.1425 in the Greek: "got to emphasize the Tragic. The *EI* beginning of worry & later madness. Contrast of O. & E. from now on."

1711 *They don't*: In **TMS** Pound wondered about the tone of the Greek at 1.1453: "OUK?? completely sarcastic. in which case she not Apios [ἠπίως 1.1439] as chorus advised."

1724 s.d.: A diagram by Pound in **TMS** suggests a large "double door" would be opened here as opposed to an inset "small door" made for "ordinary use."

1729 *and not wait till they're dead*: Pound apparently grew impatient with the Greek at 11.1460ff. **TMS** notes: "SYNTAX gorDAMMMit."

1732 *that's a shape*: Pound suggested in **FC**: "i.e. under the sheet."

1780 *from your father*: Fleming typed in **FC**: "(The idea is that Agamemnon had been notably lacking in foresight?)"

ATWOOD LIBRARY / BEAVER COLLEGE
PA4414.E5 P68 1989   MAIN
Sophocles/Elektra : a play

3 3295 00087 6000

PA 4414 .E5 P68 1989
Sophocles.
Elektra

DATE DUE

BEAVER COLLEGE LIBRARY
GLENSIDE. PA. 19038

DEMCO